| CONDENSED |

CAMBRIDGESHIRE
LIBRARIES
WITHDRAWN
FROM STOCK
SOLD

 sally o'brien

LONELY PLANET PUBLICATIONS
Melbourne • Oakland • London • Paris

contents

Madrid Condensed: 1st edition – March 2003

Published by
Lonely Planet Publications Pty Ltd
ABN 36 005 607 983
90 Maribyrnong St, Footscray, Vic 3011, Australia
|e| www.lonelyplanet.com or AOL keyword: lp

Lonely Planet offices
Australia Locked Bag 1, Footscray, Vic 3011
         ☎ 03 8379 8000 fax 03 8379 8111
         |e| talk2us@lonelyplanet.com.au
USA   150 Linden St, Oakland, CA 94607
         ☎ 510 893 8555 Toll Free 800 275 8555
         fax 510 893 8572
         |e| info@lonelyplanet.com
UK   10a Spring Place, London NW5 3BH
         ☎ 020 7428 4800 fax 020 7428 4828
         |e| go@lonelyplanet.co.uk
France   1 rue du Dahomey, 75011 Paris
         ☎ 01 55 25 33 00 fax 01 55 25 33 01
         |e| bip@lonelyplanet.fr
         www.lonelyplanet.fr

Designer Steven Cann Editor Simone Egger Proofer
Adrienne Costanzo Cartographers Andrew Smith,
Jacqui Nguyen, Jarrad Needham & Tony Fankhauser
Cover Designers Annika Roojun & Gerilyn Attebery
Project Manager Charles Rawlings-Way Commission-
ing Editor Heather Dickson Series Designer Gerilyn
Attebery Series Publishing Managers Katrina Browning
& Diana Saad Thanks to LPI, Nikki Anderson & Rowan
McKinnon

Photographs
All uncredited photos by Guy Moberly. Other images
as indicated.

Many of the photographs in this guide are available
for licensing from Lonely Planet Images:
|e| www.lonelyplanetimages.com
Edward Hopper's 'Hotel Room' image on p17 used
with kind permission of Museo Thyssen-Bornemisza.

Front cover photographs
Top Hats near Puerta del Sol (Christopher Wood)
Bottom Torres Puerta Europa (Donald C. & Pricilla
Alexander Eastman)

ISBN 1 74059 392 8

Text & maps © Lonely Planet Publications Pty Ltd 2003
Grateful acknowledgement is made to World Food
Spain, and for reproduction permission of Metro de
Madrid: Madrid Metro Map ©2001
Photos © photographers as indicated
Printed through Colorcraft Ltd, Hong Kong
Printed in China

All rights reserved. No part of this publication may
be reproduced, stored in a retrieval system or
transmitted in any form by any means, electronic,
mechanical, photocopying, recording or otherwise,
except brief extracts for the purpose of review,
without the written permission of the publisher.
Lonely Planet, the Lonely Planet logo, Lonely Planet
Images, CitySync and ekno are trademarks of Lonely
Planet Publications Pty Ltd. Other trademarks are the
property of their respective owners.

Although the authors and Lonely Planet try to make the
information as accurate as possible, we accept no
responsibility for any loss, injury or inconvenience
sustained by anyone using this book.

facts about madrid

Wanna wake up in a city that never sleeps? Then this is your town. Madrid is like a heady, frothy beer slammed down in front of you. It's sometimes accompanied by a dazzling smile or studied indifference, but always with a small plate of tempting titbits pushed towards you.

This is a place where people aren't fazed by out-of-towners (after all, Madrid's population is full to bursting with people who weren't born here) and pride themselves on an 'anything goes' attitude to other peoples' lives. The harsh repression of the Franco years saw an explosion of extroverted creativity and festivity upon his de-

mise in 1975, and *madrileños* (citizens of Madrid) aren't about to look backwards. Don't be surprised by animated conversations between strangers being struck up around you – join in. Self-consciousness and 'knowing one's place' are not the norm here – enjoying life is, whether it be at a sun-drenched *terraza* (terrace), a spine-tingling flamenco performance, a bloody bullfight, a fevered soccer match, a long lunch, a quick tapas stop, a soul-stirring day in an art museum, early morning dancing in a nightclub or a colourful local fiesta.

With the hours they keep, at first you'll wonder how madrileños have time for business, but you'll soon realise that their business *is* pleasure, and the city's infrastructure has been set up to accommodate this in many ways. As the old saying goes: 'Work to live – don't live to work'. And no other city lives quite like Madrid.

Whose shout? Café Central (p94)

HISTORY
Muslim Influence
Magerit, or Mayrit, as it came to be known, was a fortified garrison against the small Christian kingdoms to the north from 854 until well into the 10th century. Very little evidence survives, although the area between La Latina and the Palacio Real is still known as the *morería*, or Moorish quarter. Magerit was handed over to Christian rule in 1085 in exchange for the preferred area of Valencia.

Royals vs Reality
The royal court sat in Madrid for the first time in 1309, but it wasn't until 1561 that Madrid became the capital of Spain. The place still had unpaved lanes and filthy alleys, and suffered in comparison to other cities of Europe. It had no navigable river, or substantial port, and trade and communications with the rest of the country were difficult. The royal court spent untold sums on its sumptuous existence in an attempt to retreat from the squalid reality that surrounded it. The population swelled with immigrants hoping to gain patronage or a post with the machinery of government.

Caped Crusader
Carlos III's unpopular Italian minister, Esquilache, tried to have long capes declared illegal, arguing that Madrid's cleaner streets rendered them obsolete. After long riots, the notion was repealed, only to be reintroduced peacefully under a less controversial minister!

The mid-1700s was marked by a change in ruling dynasty and resulted in a period of common-sense government, with Carlos III at the helm. Madrid was generally cleaned up and attention turned to public works (with the completion of the Palacio Real and inauguration of the Jardín Botánico) and a fostering of the intellectual life of the city.

Napoleonic Interlude
Around 1805, France and Spain conspired to take Portugal. By 1808 the resulting French presence had become an occupation and Napoleon's brother was crowned king.

On 2 May 1808 townspeople attacked French troops around the Palacio Real and what is now Plaza del Dos de Mayo. The rebels were soundly defeated, but it marked the beginning of the War of Independence, a long campaign to oust the French. In 1812, 30,000 madrileños perished from hunger alone. By 1813, the war (with help from the British and Portuguese) ended.

A Republic or Civil War?
The first attempt at a republic was in 1873. The army had other ideas though, and restored the monarchy. A period of relative stability ensued and it wasn't until 1931 that a second republic was called.

By 1931, the rise of Madrid's socialists and anarchists elsewhere in Spain sharpened social tensions. A coalition of republicans and socialists proclaimed the second republic, which led to some reforms and political confrontation. Street violence and divisions within the left helped a right-wing coalition to power in 1933. Then, in 1936, it was the left-wing Frente Popular's turn to be in power. A violent face-off appeared to be inevitable – either the right-wing army would stage a coup, or the left would have its revolution.

The army moved first, and three years of bloody, horrendous warfare ensued. Franco's troops advanced from the south and were in the Casa de Campo (see p33) by early November 1936. The government fled, but a hastily assembled mix of recruits, sympathisers and International Brigades held firm, with fighting heaviest in the city's northwest. A battered Madrid finally fell to Franco on 28 March 1939.

There's a Bear in There

The symbol of Madrid city is a she-bear nuzzling a *madroño*, or strawberry tree (so named because its fruit resembles strawberries). The symbol is bordered by a frame bearing seven five-point stars and topped by a crown. If you don't believe us, check out the statue at Plaza de Puerta del Sol, near Calle del Carmen.

Look for real madroño trees in the plaza

The Franco Era

In the dark years of Franco's dictatorship, with Western Europe at war, the right-wing Falangist party maintained a heavy-handed repression, at its harshest in the 1940s. Thousands of people suspected of sympathising with the left were harassed, imprisoned and subjected to forced labour.

Spain was internationally isolated, which lead to the *años de hambre* (the years of hunger). Only in 1955 did the average wage again reach the level of 1934. By this time, discontent was expressed in the universities and workers' organisations.

The Cold War saw the US grant economic aid to Franco's Spain in exchange for the use of Spanish air and naval bases. An economic boom followed in the 1960s, but clandestine opposition to Franco's rule remained.

Return to Democracy

When Franco died in 1975 trade union and opposition groups emerged from hiding. By 1977 these groups were legalised and elections were held. A centre-right coalition won power, which set about writing a new constitution in collaboration with the opposition. It provided for a parliamentary monarchy with no state religion and guaranteed a degree of devolution of power to the 17 regions into which the country is now divided.

ORIENTATION

Madrid is surprisingly compact. The main north-south artery, Paseo de la Castellana (which becomes Paseo de los Recoletos and Paseo del Prado at its southern end) connects the city's main train stations – Chamartín and Atocha.

The core of the oldest quarters is between Paseo del Prado (east) and the Palacio Real (west). Plaza Mayor is just west of the Puerta del Sol. South of this is the working-class *barrio* of Lavapiés – a vibrant, fascinating district.

West of Lavapiés is La Latina, a slightly more polished version of Lavapiés and a popular night haunt. The most delightful part of the old quarter is just east of the palace, an area known as Los Austrias.

North of Gran Vía, which runs north-east from Plaza de la Cibeles to Plaza de España are the lively 19th-century, slightly grungy *barrios* of Chueca and Malasaña.

East of Paseo de la Castellana are the tony 19th-century neighbourhoods of Retiro (the green oasis of Madrid) and Salamanca, with wide, tree-lined streets and smart shops.

Addressing the Problem

Addresses are frequently abbreviated in Madrid. Here's a key to deciphering some of the most common usages:

Av or Avda	Avenida
C/	Calle
Gta	Glorieta (roundabout)
P° or Po	Paseo (parade/avenue)
Pl or Plz	Plaza
Pte	Puente (bridge)
s/n	*sin número* (without a number)
2°, 3° etc	2nd, 3rd floor etc

ENVIRONMENT

The usual big-city problems of air pollution are present, despite the fact that many of the streets in Madrid's older quarters have restrictions on parking and driving. The best solution for expanding your lungs with something other than traffic fumes is to head to one of Madrid's larger parks, such as the Parque del Buen Retiro or the Casa de Campo.

Plastic – not native to Río Manzanares

Rubbish disposal and collection remain a rather haphazard affair. Large, brightly coloured containers are scattered about the city for separated rubbish collection, but it's up to the locals to make use of it!

Noise pollution is a chronic problem for Madrid's citizens and visitors. Traffic, late-night partying and rubbish collection, sirens, loud conversations across inner courtyards in apartment blocks and barking dogs all assault the ears. Despite numerous protests by residents in town (look for the banners hanging off apartment balconies near the 'party plazas'), madrileños are frequently subjected to noise levels of around 80 decibels or more.

GOVERNMENT & POLITICS

Three governments rule from Madrid. The national government sits in the *cortes* (parliament), divided into the Congreso de los Diputados (lower house) on Carrera de San Jerónimo and the Senado (senate) on Plaza de España.

The city government, or *ayuntamiento*, is led by the mayor (*alcalde*) – the Partido Popular's (PP's) José Maria Alvarez del Manzano in 2002. Elections are due in 2003, with the main opposition, the Partido Socialista Obrero Español (PSOE; Spanish Socialist Workers' Party) looking strong as we went to press. The PP candidate is Alberto Ruiz-Gallardón.

> ### Did You Know?
> • Madrid's population is 3.03 million
> • The average annual salary in Madrid is €19,413
> • Madrid is the highest capital city in Europe at 650.7m above sea level

The regional government also sits in Madrid. Until the death of Franco, the province of Madrid remained a part of Castilla La Nueva (New Castile), the predecessor of today's Castilla-La Mancha. With 1983's devolution, Madrid province became a separate autonomous region, governed by a council (*consejo gobierno*), whose actions are controlled by the regional parliament (Asamblea de Madrid). Its president in 2002 was the PP's Alberto Ruiz-Gallardón.

For administrative purposes, Madrid is divided into 21 districts, each with its own local council *(junta municipal).*

ECONOMY

Madrid and its surrounding region are home to a big range of farming and industrial activities. Crops of wheat, barley, corn, garlic and grapes (among others), plus livestock, boost agriculture. Principal industries include metallurgy, chemicals, textiles, tobacco, paper and some foodstuffs. As the Spanish capital, Madrid itself is largely given over to services and big business. It's worth keeping in mind that Madrid was slow to develop during what was for many other cities the Industrial Revolution, and only really developed a middle class from the 1830s onwards.

Eternal rival Barcelona has watched with dismay as Madrid appears to grow in stature and become the prime financial and economic mover of Spain, shedding its previous image as a bureaucratic deadweight. Although unemployment fell steeply in the

Detail of the Stock Exchange building

second half of the 1990s, it still outstrips EU averages, and while the Spanish economy has been doing well in the 21st century, rising house prices are forcing the average madrileño family to spend 62% of its income on housing purchases.

SOCIETY & CULTURE

Madrid receives huge numbers of tourists every year, but it doesn't seem to phase the locals one bit. You'll find many people who speak English, particularly in the hotel and restaurant trade, but even a smattering of Spanish (officially known as *castellano*) will be patiently and warmly received, so learn a few basic phrases and don't be shy.

Born & Bred

True-blue, dyed-in-the-wool madrileños are known as *castizos* or *chulapos* (generally abbreviated to *chulos* – although the word can have some negative connotations, so perhaps it's best not to bandy it about). Occasionally you'll hear working-class men and women of Lavapiés referred to as *manolos* and *manolas* respectively.

About 185,000 migrants live in the city: Ecuadorians, Colombians and Moroccans comprise the majority, with Pakistanis, Africans, Chinese and Latin Americans filling the ranks. Many 'madrileños' also hail from elsewhere in Spain, making for a lively mix of cultures and accents.

Most madrileños profess to be Catholic, although this is often little more than lip service on a day-to-day basis. Still, passion remains strong for Easter processions and local fiestas for patron saints.

Etiquette

Madrileños can be economical with etiquette such as *por favor* and *gracias*, but don't take this as a sign of rudeness. That said, it's customary when in a bar or small shop to wish everyone a hearty *'Buenas días'* when you enter and *'Adiós'* when you leave. It's perfectly acceptable to attract the attention of the waiter or barstaff with *'oigo'* (literally, 'hear me') and the norm to respond to thanks with *'de nada'* (it's nothing).

The standard form of greeting between men and women is a light kiss on each cheek, from right to left. Men seem to take or leave handshakes on informal occasions, but they're pretty much standard in a business context. Women who are meeting for the first time – except in business situations – will generally kiss each cheek.

The Spanish concept of time is more relaxed than some other countries, but things that need a fixed time get one and it's generally adhered to. Littering is the norm, and in bars it's perfectly acceptable to chuck paper, toothpicks, cigarette butts etc onto the floor, but it's best to suss out what others are doing first.

Los Gatos (cats) - the place, not the order

ARTS
Architecture

Madrid is bereft of signs of the earlier stages of Spain's architectural history. Only a stretch of wall remains to indicate Madrid's status of early Muslim outpost, and the bell towers of the Iglesia de San Pedro El Viejo and Iglesia de San Nicolás de los Servitas are the only survivors of the Mudéjar style, which features a preponderance of brickwork. The much-interfered-with Casa de los Lujanes is the sole example of late-Gothic architecture.

Juan de Herrera (1530–97) was the greatest figure of the Spanish Renaissance, and developed a style that bears almost no resemblance to anything else of the period. His great masterpiece was the palace-monastery complex of San Lorenzo de El Escorial. Even after his death, Herrera's style lived on in Madrid. Termed *barroco madrileño* (Madrid baroque), his stern style is fused with a timid approach to the voluptuous ornamentation inherent in the baroque period. Buildings that fall into this category include the Real Casa de la Panadería, the Basilica de San Isidro, the *ayuntamiento* (town hall) and the Convento de la Encarnación. The last two were designed by Juan Gómez de Mora (1586–1648).

One of Madrid's greatest architects of the late 18th century was Ventura Rodríguez (1717–85), who designed the interior of the Convento de la Encarnación and the Palacio de Liria, in a style heading towards neoclassicism. His main competitor was the Italian Francesco Sabatini (1722–97), who finished the Palacio Real.

Neoclassicism was best executed by Juan de Villanueva (1739–1811), who designed the building now called the Museo del Prado. The 19th century saw the use of iron and glass becoming more commonplace – best exemplified by the Palacio de Cristal and train stations. The neo-Mudéjar style became *the* style for bullrings, with Las Ventas, finished in 1934, a prime example.

In the 1920s, the newly created Gran Vía provided the perfect opportunity for new building, and a number of Art Deco caprices still line the boulevard.

Madrid is a relatively modern city, which means that much of it has been constructed in the last 100 years or so. Still, few recent edifices display the sparkle of 'great architecture', although the leaning Torres Puerta Europa on Plaza de Castilla demonstrate some bold experimentation.

Palacio Real ceiling – a real palace

Painting

Madrid wasn't a centre of artistic production until 1561, when Felipe II moved the royal court here. Even so, the bulk of artists who lived and worked here came from elsewhere. Perhaps the most extraordinary of these was the Cretan-born Domenikos Theotokopoulos (1541–1614), popularly known as El Greco. He chose, however, to settle in Toledo and met with relative indifference from the court of Felipe II.

The golden age of Spanish art had few figures from Madrid, although there's plenty of great art from this period to see in the city. An extensive collection of José de Ribera's (1591–1652) works are in the Prado, as are some from Bartolomé Esteban Murillo (1618–82), while Francisco de Zurbarán's (1598–1664) work can be seen in the Real Academia de Bellas Artes de San Fernando. The great star of this time, however, was Velázquez (1599–1660), who moved to Madrid to be court painter. His eye for light and detail, plus the humanity that he captured in his subjects, are unmatched. His works can be seen at the Prado, including the masterpieces *Las Meninas* and *La Rendición de Breda*.

A parade of late-baroque artists working over the course of the 17th century has been loosely lumped together as the Madrid School, with some of them actually born and raised in Madrid.

Velázquez outside Museo del Prado – oh the humanity!

Antonio de Pereda (1608–78) and Fray Juan Rizi (1600–81) both have paintings in the Real Academia de Bellas Artes de San Fernando, while madrileño Claudio Coello (1642–93) has large-scale works displayed in San Lorenzo de El Escorial.

The 18th century saw Bohemian Anton Raphael Mengs (1728–79) as court painter, and it was his encouragement that inspired Francisco José de Goya y Lucientes (1746–1828) to begin a long and varied career. Goya is recognised as Spain's greatest artist of the 18th (and even the 19th) century. His early pieces had some of the candour of Hogarth and betrayed the influence of Tiepolo. He was appointed Carlos IV's court painter in 1799, and his style grew increasingly merciless. Masterpieces at the Prado by Goya include *La Maja Vestida* and *La Maja Desnuda* (see p15), along with *Los Caprichos* (The Caprices), a biting series of 80 etchings lambasting court life.

Madrid-born Juan Gris (1887–1927) flew the Cubist flag during his short life, and while the 20th century's greatest artist Pablo Picasso (1881–1973) was born in Málaga, he did study in Madrid for a time at the Escuela de Bellas Artes de San Fernando from 1897 (it didn't thrill him though). His most powerful work, *Guernica*, can be seen in the Centro de Arte Reina Sofía.

highlights

With some of the world's truly great museums (which are reason enough for coming), buildings that span the centuries, and atmospheric neighbourhoods brimming with character, Madrid has plenty of sights to keep you occupied. The highlights listed here are a combination of absolute must-sees and a few lesser-known favourites. Madrid's compact nature and excellent metro system are great for visitors.

Stopping Over?

Day One Take Madrid's pulse at Plaza de la Puerta del Sol, then listen to its heartbeat at Plaza Mayor. Spend at least half a day at the Museo del Prado before lunching at a traditional restaurant in the Los Austrias area. After lunch, take a walk in Campo del Moro before visiting the Palacio Real. Start the night sampling some tapas at any of the bars in Huertas and around Plaza de Santa Ana.

Day Two Start the day with a tour of Real Monasterio de las Descalzas Reales before heading to the Museo Thyssen-Bornemisza for a few hours. Refuel in Salamanca, then stroll through the Parque del Buen Retiro. Indulge in a glass of cava (champagne) at Café del Círculo de Bellas Artes before an evening stroll among the twinkling lights and grand buildings of Gran Vía.

> ### Madrid Lowlights
>
> Every city has its bits and pieces that it and you could do without – here are the things we didn't dig:
>
> - the pimps and customers of the hookers on Calle de la Montera, just off Puerta del Sol
> - the crowds on 'Free for EU citizens' Wednesday and Sunday
> - roadworks, roadworks, roadworks
> - the August exodus of locals
> - good local bars polluted by *tragaperras* – pokie machines
> - noise pollution and the lax attitude to street litter

Day Three Time for the Centro de Arte Reina Sofía, followed by a walk through the authentically gritty Lavapiés *barrio* and La Latina, over to the Basílica de San Francisco El Grande. Take lunch at one of Chueca's smart restaurants, then a post-prandial chill-out session is in order at the Real Jardín Botánico. When it starts to get dark, head to Malasaña for dinner and drinks.

Caminan en el Campo del Moro

MUSEO DEL PRADO (3, H14)

In a city with three truly great art museums, the Museo del Prado sits at the top of the heap for most visitors – indeed, the Prado is a reason in itself for many to come to Madrid. Don't despair if you feel as though you haven't absorbed everything in this extraordinary collection – common wisdom suggests you need more than one visit here, and at *least* four hours on your first!

The building itself – completed in 1785 – served as a natural history museum and laboratories, and as a cavalry barracks before its conversion in 1819 as a repository of Spanish art held in royal collections. The collection has over 7000 works, with less than half on display. A grand extension (to be completed in late 2003 at a cost of €43 million) will allow visitors greater access to the treasures.

The Prado's three floors are organised as follows: the ground floor contains 12th- to 16th-century Spanish painting, 15th- to 16th-century Flemish and German painting, 14th- to 17th-century Italian painting, and sculpture from Ancient Greece and Rome; the 1st floor contains 17th- to 18th-century Spanish painting and 17th-century Flemish, Dutch and French painting; the 2nd floor has 18th-century Spanish, British, French, German and Italian painting, with sculpture, drawings and exhibition rooms. If your time is very limited, the strongest collections are the 17th- and 18th-century Spanish paintings.

Highlights of the ground floor include the *Annunciation* by Fra Angelico, and *The Story of Nastagio degli Onesti* – a perplexing work by

The pillars of artistic integrity

- the Casón del Buen Retiro (the one-time ballroom)
- rehydrating and resting in the cafeteria

Sandro **Botticelli** – both in Room 49. *The Triumph of Death* by Pieter **Brueghel** the Elder, *The Garden of Earthly Delights* by Hieronymous **Bosch** (El Bosco in Castillian) reside in Room 56a. *Auto da fé with Saint Domenic of Guzmán* by Pedro **de Gerruguete** is in Room 57b, **Titian's** *Danaé and the Shower of Gold* in Room 61b, and **Tintoretto's** *Christ Washing the Disciples' Feet* in Room 75. The works of **El Greco** can be seen in Rooms 60a, 61a and 62a; of particular note is his striking *Crucifixion*.

On the 1st floor, unmissables abound: *Atalanta and Hippomenes* by Guido **Reni** is in Room 5 (see also Plaza de la Cibeles, p31), and *The Three Graces* by **Rubens** in Room 9. *Christ Embracing Saint Bernard* by Francisco **de Ribalta** hangs in Room 24, and José **de Ribera's** sweet-eyed *Magdalen* is in Room 25. A collection of **Velázquez'** paintings (that any museum would kill for) is housed in Room 12; his innovative depic-

INFORMATION

✉ Edificio Villanueva, Paseo del Prado
☎ 91 330 28 00
@ http://museoprado.mcu.es
Ⓜ Banco de España
🕐 Tues-Sat 9am-7pm, Sun & hols 9am-2pm; closed 1 Jan, Good Friday, 1 May & 25 Dec
💲 adult/concession €3/1.50
ⓘ booklets €1
♿ good
🍴 cafeteria and restaurant

tion of *The Triumph of Bacchus* competes with *Las Meninas*, which is perhaps the most extraordinary painting of the 17th century. It depicts Velázquez himself (on the left) painting a portrait (it is assumed) of King Felipe IV and Mariana of Austria (visible in the mirror) while the Infanta Margarita and her *meninas* (maids) enter the room, in the company of dwarves. Cheeky Velázquez depicts himself with the cross of the Order of Santiago on his breast – years before it was granted to him. The mathematical composition of the painting and use of perspective is a singular great achievement in Spanish painting. Other works by Velázquez are in Rooms 14, 15, 15a and 16.

Masterpieces by **Goya** can also be found on the 1st floor (Rooms 32 & 34–9). These last rooms contain his haunting *Pinturas Negras* (Black Paintings), including the truly disturbing *Saturn Devouring his Children* (Room 39). Also in Room 39 are *The 2nd of May* and *The 3rd of May*, which portray the 1808 anti-French revolt in Madrid and the repercussions of it, respectively. On the 2nd floor, which devotes its whole southern wing to Goya, you'll find the charming *La Maja Vestida* and *La Maja Desnuda*, both portraits of the same woman – one clothed, one nude.

 DON'T MISS
• the *Tesoro del Delfín* in the basement
• suss out the copyists replicating the masters

MUSEO THYSSEN-BORNEMISZA   (3, G13)

In 1994, Madrid succeeded in getting the art collection that everyone wanted: that of Baron Thyssen-Bornemisza – an avid and voracious collector of predominantly European art who was happiest when buying a painting a week! The neoclassical Palacio de Villahermosa was overhauled to house the 800-odd piece collection, and in 2000 two adjoining buildings were acquired to hold a further 300 paintings, which should be open by late 2004.

Start perusing the collection on the 2nd floor, where you'll find a remarkable series of medieval triptychs and paintings of Italian, German and Flemish origin; Room 3's minuscule *Our Lady of the Dry Tree* demands a closer look. Room 4 highlights 15th-century Italian art, including works by Paolo **Uccello** (1397–1475). Hans **Holbein** the Younger's (1497–1543) wonderful *Henry VIII* can be found in Room 5 among an assortment of early Renaissance portraiture. Room 6 (known as the Villahermosa Gallery) hosts a sampling of Italian masters such as Lorenzo **Lotto** (c 1480–1556), **Raphael** (1483–1520), **Titian** (c 1490–1576) and **Tintoretto** (1518–94), and a darkly beautiful *Saint Casilda* by **Zurbarán**. Rooms 7 to 10 are devoted to 16th-century works from Italy, Germany, and the Netherlands. Four pieces by **El Greco** are displayed in Room 11, while a wonderful portrait of *Saint Catherine of Siena* by **Caravaggio** (whose influence on José de Ribera is obvious) is in Room 12. Rooms 13 to 15 display Italian, French and Spanish works of the 17th century, followed by 18th-century Italian work in Rooms 16 to 18, with some wonderful views of Venice by **Canaletto** (1697–1768). **Rubens'** *The Toilet of Venus* dominates the 17th-century works of Flemish, Dutch and German origin found in Rooms 19 to 21, with Anton **van Dyck**, Jan **Brueghel** and **Rembrandt** also represented.

Baron Hans Heinrich Thyssen-Bornemisza

The good baron, one of *the* great art collectors, died on 27 April 2002. In 1993, he wrote: 'An artist's talent is a gift to the world. When I began my collection, my eyes were my principal asset, and these are a gift from God. Painters do not create their works for one person alone. My legacy as a collector is to share my collection and I can only return God's gift by making it possible for more than one person to see it and to appreciate the artist's talent'. There's a full-length portrait of the baron on the museum's ground floor – don't forget to say thanks!

The 1st floor continues with the 17th-century Dutch theme from Rooms 22 to 26, with some still lifes in Room 27. Room 18 gives 18th-century art a look-in with **Gainsborough** (1727–88). Other continental artists from before the 19th century (North American and European) take over Rooms 29 to 31, with John Singer **Sargent** (1856–1925), John **Constable** (1776–1837) and Gustave **Courbet** (1819–77). Lovers of impressionism and post-impressionist works will be delighted by the museum's collection in Rooms 32 to 33, with paintings by **Renoir**

(1841–1919), **Degas** (1834–1917), **Manet** (1832–83), **Monet** (1840–1926) and **Van Gogh** (1853–90). Then, in a flurry of colour, Rooms 34 to 40 highlight Fauvist and Expressionist art in all their coruscating brilliance, with Egon **Schiele** (1890–1918), Henri **Matisse** (1869–1954), Edvard **Munch** (1863–1944) and **The Blue Rider** school (1911–14) founded by Wassily Kandinsky.

INFORMATION

✉ Paseo del Prado 8
☎ 91 369 01 51
ⓔ www.museothyssen
   .org
Ⓜ Banco de España
🕐 Tues-Sun 10am-7pm
💲 adult/concession
   €4.80/3, temporary
   exhibitions
   €3.60/2.40,
   combined ticket
   €6.60/3.60,
   free under-12
ⓘ guided handsets €3
♿ excellent
✕ cafeteria

On the ground floor, visitors are given a powerful dose of the 20th century, from cubism to pop art. The experimental avant-gardes have commandeered Rooms 41 to 44, with **Picasso** (1881–1973) and Juan **Gris** (1887–1927) flying the Spanish flag, and Georges **Braque**. In Room 45, European expressionism prepares you for the next room's focus on works from the USA, with paintings by Jackson **Pollock** (1912–56), a stunning Mark **Rothko** (1903–70) and Georgia **O'Keefe** (1887–1980). For the last two rooms, it's late-surrealism to pop art, with one of our faves from Room 47 being Edward **Hopper's** *Hotel Room*. Lucien **Freud's** wonderful *Portrait of Baron Thyssen-Bornemisza* in Room 48 gives the visitor a chance to compare the complexity of the sitter's face as depicted here with the full-length portrait of the museum's namesake hanging near the entrance.

Part of the pleasure of a visit here lies in the methodical organisation and layout of the museum, which is easy to navigate and therefore makes it easy to appreciate its treasures. There are also such thoughtfully amusing touches as the fact that even the 'no smoking' signs are small canvases!

COPYRIGHT © Edward Hopper, 2002
Provenance: Museo Thyssen-Bornemisza

'Hotel Room' by Edward Hopper

CENTRO DE ARTE REINA SOFÍA   (2, O5)

The expansive Centro de Arte Reina Sofía was adapted from the remains of the 18th-century San Carlos hospital with the intention of presenting the best Madrid has to offer in 20th-century Spanish art. The occasional appearance of non-Spanish artworks provides some useful comparisons between the Iberian works and the outside world. The museum's position in bohemian Lavapiés contrasts nicely with such space-age touches as the shiny steel-and-glass external elevators.

The museum's permanent collection is displayed over the 2nd and 4th floors. The 1st and 3rd floors are used to stage some excellent temporary exhibitions, and the 1st floor also boasts a bookshop and pleasant cafeteria.

Floor Plan Tips

The Centro de Arte Reina Sofia uses the US-style floor numbering system, which can cause a little confusion for first-time visitors. All you need to keep in mind is that the ground floor is known as the *primera planta* (1st floor) and so on.

Room 1 (2nd floor) gives visitors an introduction to Spanish painting at the turn of the 20th century, which tended to be dominated by the Barcelona scene. Among the artists featured are Santiago **Rusiñol** (1861–1931), Ramón **Casas** (1866–1932), and Isidro **Nonell** (1873–1911), along with the important Basque painter Ignazio **Zuloaga** (1870–1945).

Room 2 concentrates on *madrileño* José Gutiérrez **Solana** (1886–1945), whose dark-hued *La Tertulia de Café de Pombo* depicts an intellectual gossip session typical of 1920s Madrid. Room 3 presents a mix of Spanish and foreign painters whose work came before, during and after cubism, best exemplified by the works of Juan **Gris** in Room 4. Bronze and iron sculptures by Pablo **Gargallo** (1881–1934) are on display in Room 5.

The massive Room 6 is devoted to **Picasso** and dominated by the extraordinary *Guernica*. The painting (which is the sole reason many visitors come to this museum) is surrounded by a plethora of Picasso's preparatory sketches, and was commissioned by Spain's republican government for the Paris Exposition Universelle in 1937. That was the year that the German Condor Legion (working for Nationalist forces) bombed the Basque town of Gernika (Guernica), provoking outrage in Spain and abroad. The 3.5 by 7.8m painting, which Picasso did not want in Spain during the Franco dictatorship, was only returned from the USA in 1981. The breathtaking force of the work, the fact that it's one of the most famous paintings of the 20th century – and one of the starkest depictions of war's brutality – leaves much of the museum's collection for dust.

After such an experience, Room 7 showcases the primary-coloured works of Joan **Miró** (1893–1983), which are interspersed with a collection of twisting bronzes (and some sketches) by Juan **González** (1876–1942). Those with a penchant for surrealist extravaganzas will love Room 10, with Salvador **Dalí's** (1904–1989) *The Great Masturbator* (1929) and the disconcertingly straightforward *Girl at the Window* (1925). Rooms 11 and 12 have other surrealist works, including films by filmmaker Luis **Buñuel**, while Room 13 hosts works by artists active in the turbulent 1920s and

1930s. Luis **Fernández**, Benjamin **Palencia** and sculptor Alberto **Sánchez** are represented in Rooms 14 and 15, with Joan **Miró** sculptures in Room 16.

The 4th floor comprises artworks created after the civil war – in an atmosphere of Francoist repression – to the present day, starting with Juan Manuel Diáz **Caneja** (1905–1988) landscapes in Room 18. In Room 19, works by two important post-WWII groups are presented – Pórtico and Dau al Set. Barcelona's Antoni **Tápies** (born in 1923) is one artist from the latter group – his textural explorations are worth noting. Abstract

INFORMATION

✉ Calle de Santa Isabel 52
☎ 91 467 50 62
e http://museoreina sofia.mcu.es
Ⓜ Atocha
🕐 Wed-Sat & Mon 10am-9pm, Sun 10am-2.30pm
Ⓢ adult/concession €3/1.50
ⓘ guided handsets €2.40
♿ excellent
✕ cafeteria

painting comes to the fore from Rooms 20 to 23, with members of the Equipo 57 group on display. From Room 24, the 1960s and 1970s are given an airing, with foreign references provided by Francis **Bacon** and Henry **Moore**. The present day, from Room 38, is given over to works by Eduardo **Arroya**, while sculptures by Eduardo **Chillida** fill Rooms 42 and 43.

The great glass elevators of Centro de Arte Reina Sofía

PLAZA MAYOR (3, G8)

The Puerta del Sol may feel like the hub of Madrid, but its imperial heart beats loudest at Plaza Mayor – the town square designed in 1619 by Juan Gómez de Mora. In the Middle Ages this area was positioned outside the city walls and known as Plaza del Arrabal. Traders liked the location as it enabled them to peddle their wares free from intramural taxation. The *alhóndiga del pan* – where wheat and flour to make bread were sold – was located here (to be replaced by the **Real Casa de la Panadería**, or royal bakery) along with butchers' stalls, fishmongers, wine stores and more. There are still plenty of shops in the plaza, and they're often good places to pick up local craft objects.

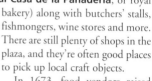

INFORMATION

Ⓜ Sol
ⓘ Tourist office at No 3
♿ good
✕ See Los Austrias
   pp82-3

In 1673, food vendors raised tarpaulins above their stalls, thus protecting their wares (and themselves) from the refuse that people habitually tossed out of their windows from above. A fire in 1790 destroyed much of the plaza, but with Juan de Villanueva's supervision, a more-or-less faithful reproduction was soon delivered to the people of Madrid.

In the past, the plaza was the site of royal festivities, autos-da-fé (the ritual condemnation and burning of heretics) and bullfights. These days it's largely given over to those fancying an alfresco drink or snack, or wanting to meet up with people in an obvious location (some get really specific – 'under the testicles of the sculpted horse that Felipe III sits astride'). And if you think the murals adorning the Real Casa de la Panadería look a little modern, you're right. They're a 1990s addition, and a surprising success.

Felipe III oversees Plaza Mayor from atop his horse

DON'T MISS
- a morning coffee at any of the cafés
- the Sunday morning stamp and coin collectors' market
- buying a lurid 'your name here' bullfighting poster

PALACIO REAL   (3, F5)

Madrid's alcazar (fortress) burned down in 1734, giving King Felipe V the chance to really make his mark in the city with a dose of architectural splendour.

Felipe didn't live long enough to see the fruits of architects Filippo Juvara and Giovanni Batista Sacchetti's labours. Construction of the Italianate baroque palace lasted 26 years, by which time King Carlos III was in charge, and much of the palace's interior reflects his predilections. There are 2800 rooms, of which you can visit around 50.

Access to the apartments is from the northern end of Plaza de la Armería, where you'll ascend the grand stairway to the **Halberdier's rooms**, before entering the sumptuous blood-red and gold **Throne Room** with a Tiepolo ceiling. After this, you'll enter the **rooms of Carlos III**. His drawing room features a vault fresco, *The Apotheosis of Trajan* by Anton Raphael Mengs. The blue antechamber, decorated in the neoclassical style also has ceiling work by Mengs, this time depicting the *Apotheosis of Hercules*; there are also four portraits by Goya.

The **Gasparini Room** features an exquisite stucco ceiling and walls of embroidered chinoiserie silk. The extraordinary **Porcelain Room** (the name says it all), has elaborate details climbing every surface. Many of the rooms are awash with a predominant colour (yellow, green, blue or red), and in the midst of such luxury comes the sumptuous **Gala Dining Room**, with seating for what seems like thousands, and some staggering examples of tapestry work.

INFORMATION

✉ Calle de Bailén
☎ 91 454 88 00
🖥 www.patrimonio nacional.es
Ⓜ Ópera
🕐 1 Apr-30 Sep Mon-Sat 9am-6pm, Sun & hols 9am-3pm; 1 Oct-31 Mar Mon-Sat 9.30am-5pm, Sun & hols 9am-2pm
💲 adult/concession €6/3, free under-5 & Wed for EU citizens
ⓘ guided tours €7
♿ good
✕ cafeteria

Imposing Palacio Real

DON'T MISS
• the Armería Real (Royal Armoury) • the Farmacia Real (Pharmacy)
• the changing of the guard (1st Wed of every month Sept-June)
• the view from Plaza de la Armería over the parkland to the west

REAL MONASTERIO DE LAS DESCALZAS REALES (3, F8)

The Real Monasterio de las Descalzas Reales is an oasis of calm in the heart of frenetic Madrid. This unmissable treasure trove of art exists thanks to Doña Juana of Austria, Felipe II's sister who converted the former palace into a Franciscan convent (there are still 23 nuns cloistered here) in the mid-16th century. She was followed by the Descalzas Reales (Barefooted Royals), a group of illustrious women who became Franciscan nuns, bringing some extraordinary works of art with them.

The convent's centre features a small garden with orange trees and a fountain, its simplicity in marked contrast to the elaborate Renaissance stairway, which features lavish fresco work and a painted vault by Claudio Coello. A portrait of Felipe II and three royal children looks down at visitors from the top of the stairs – with a suitably sombre and inbred cast to their features.

There are 33 (Christ's age at death) chapels in the convent, and a compulsory tour takes you past several of them. The first contains an eerily realistic recumbent Christ. The tombs of Doña Juana and Empress Maria of Austria are in the choir, which has 33 stalls (the convent's maximum capacity is 33 nuns). The convent also contains an extraordinary collection of 17th-century **tapestries** from Brussels, which are kept in the former sleeping quarters. Along the way, try spotting works by Rubens, Titian and Brueghel (you might need to if you're following a Spanish-language tour and don't speak Spanish).

INFORMATION

- ✉ Plaza de las Descalzas 3
- ☎ 91 542 00 59
- Ⓔ www.patrimonio nacional.es
- Ⓜ Sol or Callao
- ⏰ Tues–Thur & Sat 10.30am–12.45pm & 4–5.45pm, Fri 10.30am–12.45pm, Sun & public holidays 11am–1.45pm
- ⓢ adult/concession €3.45/1.80, free under-5 & Wed for EU citizens, combined ticket (valid 7 days) with Real Monasterio de la Encarnacion (see p40) €6/3.30
- ⓘ compulsory guided tour (English available) included in entry fee
- ✕ see Sol & Gran Vía p87

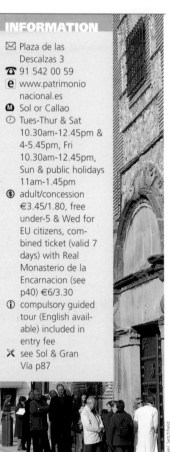

A treasure trove of art awaits

Neil Setchfield

DON'T MISS
- the Bosch-style painting of the *Ship of Salvation*
- Pedro de la Mena's *Dolorosa*

PLAZA DE LA VILLA   (3, H6)

It is thought that this plaza was chosen to be the city's permanent seat of government in the late Middle Ages. It's one of Madrid's most beautiful spots, with a sense of history and some damn fine architecture.

The oldest structure is the early-15th-century **Casa de Los Lujanes**, with an exquisite tower, Gothic portals and Mudéjar arches. The tower is said to have held the imprisoned French monarch François I and his sons after they were captured during the Battle of Pavia in 1525.

The **Casa de Cisneros** was constructed in 1537 by the nephew of Cardinal Cisneros, who was a key adviser to Queen Isabel. It is *plateresque* (Spanish Renaissance) in inspiration, although it was much restored and altered at the beginning of the 20th century. The most obvious signs of the Renaissance style are visible in the main door and window above. It now serves as the *alcalde* (mayor's office) – lucky him!

A marvellous enclosed bridge links the Casa de Cisneros building with Madrid's 17th-century **ayuntamiento** (town hall), which stands on the western side of the plaza. This building is a wonderful example of the *barroco madrileño* (Madrid baroque) style, with Herrerian slate-tile spires. It was originally planned by Juan Goméz de Mora to be a prison, but ended up serving as both a prison and a town hall.

INFORMATION

Ⓜ Ópera
ⓘ free guided tours of the *ayuntamiento* (Spanish) on Mon 5pm & 6pm (arrive 10mins before)
♿ good
✕ see Los Austrias pp82-4

Plaza de la Villa

A Tight Budget

The austere demeanour of Madrid's *ayuntamiento* is due to the scarcity of funds for municipal buildings during the 17th century. As a matter of fact the *consejo* (town council) had met for the previous three centuries in the Iglesia de San Salvador (no longer standing), which once faced the plaza on Calle Mayor.

REAL JARDÍN BOTÁNICO (3, J15)

Meticulously maintained, the real Jardín Botánico is a must-visit for those seeking some green respite. Originally created in 1755 under orders from King Fernanado VI on the banks of the Río Manzanares, the gardens consisted of over 2000 plants.

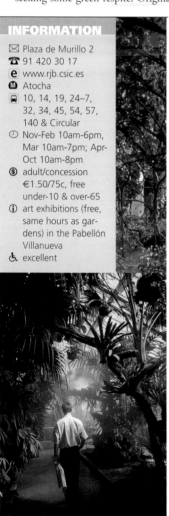

INFORMATION

- ✉ Plaza de Murillo 2
- ☎ 91 420 30 17
- ℮ www.rjb.csic.es
- Ⓜ Atocha
- 🚌 10, 14, 19, 24–7, 32, 34, 45, 54, 57, 140 & Circular
- ◷ Nov-Feb 10am-6pm, Mar 10am-7pm; Apr-Oct 10am-8pm
- ⑤ adult/concession €1.50/75c, free under-10 & over-65
- ⓘ art exhibitions (free, same hours as gardens) in the Pabellón Villanueva
- ♿ excellent

In 1774, King Carlos III decided that the garden should be moved to Paseo del Prado, which was completed in 1781. The **Pabellón Villanueva**, designed by Juan de Villanueva, was constructed and botany classes were taught here in the early 19th century. Today it is used to display free art exhibitions.

The 1808 War of Independence wasn't kind to the gardens, with little money being set aside for maintenance and development. In the 1850s though, the garden was renovated and a zoo was established (now at Buen Retiro). The enormous Ministry of Agriculture building swallowed two hectares of the garden's space (leaving a total of eight) in 1882, and a cyclone in 1886 battered over 500 trees. After generations of serious neglect, the gardens were closed to the public in 1974, and extensive renovations carried out that – after seven years – saw the gardens restored to their former glory. For some unknown reason, you'll generally encounter few people as you stroll through the charming canopied pathways, admire the plots and statues of famous botanists, and the sounds of chirping birds. At these times, the chaos of Paseo del Prado seems miles away.

Steamy Real Jardín Botánico

DON'T MISS
- The muggy Exhibition Greenhouse • The plot of old roses
- The plots of medicinal, aromatic and culinary plants

GRAN VÍA   (3, C7–E12)

Madrid's mighty boulevard cuts a southeastwards swathe through the city from Plaza de España to Calle de Alcalá. It is in parts tacky, energetic, elegant and garish. You'll find luxury hotels, *hostales,* fast-food joints, sex shops, chain stores, elegant fashion houses, banks, Internet cafés, cinemas, theatres and nightclubs, and a lot of people and vehicles!

INFORMATION

Ⓜ Plaza de España, Santo Domingo, Callao or Gran Vía

✕ see Sol & Gran Vía p87

The Gran Vía was constructed in the first decades of the 20th century, when over a dozen streets were discarded and entire neighbourhoods bulldozed, all to be replaced by grand architectural piles. Spain's neutral status in WWI made Madrid a prosperous city when other European capitals were riven with poverty.

Keep your eyes peeled for some buildings of note situated along Gran Vía (it can be tricky when there's so much throbbing life at ground level!), which provide a progressive tour through the 20th century's architectural trends. At Gran Vía 1 there's the **Edificio Grassy** (see p43). At No 2, **La Gran Peña** is a curved wedding cake of a structure. At No 10, **Edificio Estrella** is an excellent example of Madrid's ability to blend neoclassical influences, while No 12 is an Art Deco delight of a bar, the **Museo Chicote** (see p92). Gran Vía 28 is the site of Madrid's first skyscraper, the **Telefónica** building (see p45), while the intersection at Plaza Callao is rich in Art Deco-era cinemas (and human traffic!).

Gran Vía - the grand way

Big Guns

During the civil war, the length and breadth of Gran Vía made it perfect for artillery shells to thunder in from the front lines around the Ciudad Universitaria to the north. Gran Vía was subsequently nicknamed 'Howitzer Alley' (after the cannon).

PARQUE DEL BUEN RETIRO (2, N6)

Madrid's magnificent green lungs began life as the Real Sitio del Buen Retiro, or palatial grounds of King Felipe IV (1621–65). After Isabel II's ousting in 1868, the park was opened to one and all, which is exactly what you'll find on any weekend in this busy, vital and beautiful spot. Buskers,

INFORMATION

- ☺ Observatory Mon-Thur 9am-2pm, tours Fri 11am
- Ⓜ Retiro, Ibiza or Atocha
- ♿ good

hawkers, fortune-tellers, potheads, families, lovers, puppeteers, cyclists, joggers, and tourists all soak up the leisure options and add to the atmosphere – particularly on a Sunday morning, or after Sunday lunch.

The artificial lake (*estanque*) is watched over by the massive structure of Alfonso XII's mausoleum. The western side of the lake features the **Fuente Egipcia** (Egyptian fountain), where legend says a fortune was buried (unfortunately not true).

South of the lake you'll find the **Palacio de Velázquez** and the **Palacio de Cristal** (Crystal Palace), which were both built by Ricardo Velázquez Bosco. The Palacio de Cristal, a particularly charming metal-and-glass structure, was built in 1887 as a winter garden for exotic flowers. Occasional exhibitions are held here and in the Palacio de Velázquez.

The very southern part of the park's borders contains one of Madrid's loveliest examples of 18th-century architecture – the **Observatorio Astronómico** (Astronomical Observatory), designed by Juan de Villanueva for King Carlos III.

Don't throw stones in crystal palaces – the Palacio de Cristal

DON'T MISS
- the Casón del Buen Retiro – the only remnant of the original palace (see also Museo del Prado, p14)
- *El Ángel Caído* (The Fallen Angel) – a statue of Lucifer

EL RASTRO   (3, K8)

Sunday morning may seem quiet in other parts of Madrid, but in the area around Calle de Embajadores things are positively humming by 9am, buzzing by 11am and exploding by 2pm. El Rastro flea market has been given mixed coverage of late, with some believing it's not as good as it used to be, and that it caters mostly to tourists nowadays. Rubbish! On any given Sunday you'll find the streets choked with madrileños, tourists, a few pickpockets (watch your bags) and a cornucopia of stalls selling whatever you fancy – clothes, accessories, electrical goods, music, plants, furniture, art, food, drink and general junk.

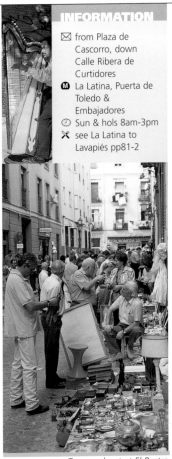

INFORMATION

✉ from Plaza de Cascorro, down Calle Ribera de Curtidores

Ⓜ La Latina, Puerta de Toledo & Embajadores

🕐 Sun & hols 8am-3pm

✕ see La Latina to Lavapiés pp81-2

The main action takes place from Plaza de Cascorro, down Calle Ribera de Curtidores, although it's always worth wandering off into the sidestreets and perusing the makeshift stalls that are set up on blankets and sheets placed on the ground. The less-transient shops of the neighbourhood are also doing a roaring trade, with second-hand shops (often specialising in particular goods) staying open on what's supposed to be a day of rest. Calle de Arganzuela, for example, seems to be *the* place if you're into military antiques and old office goods. The cafés, bars and restaurants of the neighbourhood provide sustenance for those who need re-fuelling (some of the streets are quite steep). Places to eat generally get really crowded from 2pm – when the market is at its peak and people start to think about lunch.

Treasure hunt at El Rastro

What's in a Name?
Wondering where the market gets its name from? It comes from the fact that the area was a meat market in the 17th and 18th centuries – *rastro* refers to the trail of blood left behind when animals were dragged down the hill.

CAMPO DEL MORO (2, M2)

The exquisite Campo del Moro (Moor's Field) is aptly named, as it was here that an Almoravid army, led by Ali ben Yusef, set up camp beneath Madrid's walls in 1110 in the hope of retaking the town (they were unsuccessful). In medieval times, the area was used for jousting tournaments among knights. The park was not laid out as it now appears until 1844, with further alterations in 1890, when it was used as a playground for royal children. The 20th century saw the park open to the public under the second republic of 1931, and closed under the dictatorship of Franco. King Juan Carlos I declared the park open to the public in 1983, although you could be forgiven for thinking that not everyone had been told, as this beautiful spot often seems devoid of people.

INFORMATION

- ✉ Paseo de la Virgen del Puerto
- ☎ 91 542 00 59
- Ⓜ Ópera or Príncipe Pío
- ⏱ Mon-Sat 10am-8pm, Sun & hols 9am-8pm

As you enter the park (from the gate at Paseo de la Virgen del Puerto) and head down the charming rockery stairs, aspects of the park's English style become apparent. Among all the greenery, you'll find winding paths, verdant canopies, many neatly laid-out flowerbeds and two delightful fountains. The fountain known as **Fuente de las Conchas** was designed by Ventura Rodríguez in the 18th century. The other, **Fuente de los Tritones**, was made in the 17th century for the grounds of Aranjuez. Also on the grounds is the Museo de los Carruajes (Museum of Carriages), which has been closed for some time and doesn't look like opening anytime soon.

Quiet time at Campo del Moro

DON'T MISS
- the peacocks, peahens and ducks that rule this particular roost
- the morning quiet
- inspecting the curious little English-style cabins that dot the grounds

BASÍLICA DE SAN FRANCISCO EL GRANDE (3, K4)

According to legend, Saint Francis himself built a chapel on the site of this basilica in 1217, hence the name. The present building is one of the city's biggest churches, and was completed under the watchful eye of Francesco Sabatini in 1784, after the original architect, Francesco Cabezas, had difficulty with the enormous expanse of the 33m-diameter dome. And indeed, it's an enormous place of worship, parts of which have been nicely restored in recent years.

INFORMATION

✉ Plaza de San Francisco
☎ 91 365 38 00
Ⓜ La Latina
🕐 Tues-Sat 11am-1pm & 5-7pm
⑤ 60c
✗ see La Latina to Lavapiés pp81-2

The elaborate interior decorations are the result of restoration work carried out in 1878. At the entrance, the building arcs off in both directions in a flurry of columns. Upon entering you will probably be directed to a series of corridors lined with artworks behind the church's glittering high altar. A guide will take you to the sacristy, which features fine Renaissance *sillerís* (sculpted walnut seats where the church's superiors would meet). Walnut is a feature of the church's seven doors, which were carved by Juan Guas. Take note of the lovely frescoed cupolas and chapel ceilings by Francisco Bayeu (yes, it does seem that almost everyone who worked on the building had a variation on the name of the patron saint).

The chapel on your left as you enter the building has a **Goya**

Basílica de San Francisco el Grande

painting of *The Sermon of San Bernardino of Siena*, while the adjoining chapel has a startling depiction of Christ. Extensive restoration work over the years means that a visit often includes some scaffolding.

Grande Plans
One grand 19th-century idea that never left the drawing board was the ambitious plan to create a linking plaza supported by a viaduct between the basilica and the Palacio Real. The mind boggles…

REAL MADRID (2, E6)

There may be a lot of Catholic highlights on the peninsula, but to many Real Madrid is the real sacred turf of Spain. A powerhouse of Spanish, European and international football, Real Madrid was named Team of the Century in 1998 by FIFA, and the club's list of achievements is long and impressive: 28 Spanish League titles, 17 Spanish Cup titles, 9 European Champions Cup titles and 2 UEFA Cup titles – among others.

The club celebrated its centenary in 2002 (its name was changed from Madrid Foot-Ball in 1920, thanks to King Alfonso XII), and the excitement can be savoured in a visit to the stadium, Estadio Santiago Bernabéu, named after the club's most illustrious president, who served from 1943 for 32 enviable years. While a trip to the Exposición de Trofeos (trophy exhibition) is a poor second to catching a match in the 85,000-seat stadium against arch-rivals FC Barcelona, it's much easier to organise. You'll see the silverware and some boots of note, plus a video presentation of the club's glorious victories.

Smoking is not allowed, but you definitely get the feeling that a lot of people want a post-coital cig when Queen's *We are the Champions* goes into overdrive at the conclusion of one video. Expect to be joined by excited kids, misty-eyed men and football-loving women. For about €60 you can get a Real Madrid strip (club colours) at the attached shop (if you want a strip with a name and number, you'll pay about €72).

INFORMATION

- ✉ Paseo de la Castellana 144
- ☎ Exposición de Trofeos 91 457 06 79, tickets 91 398 43 00
- e www.realmadrid.com
- Ⓜ Santiago Bernabéu
- 🚌 No 27
- 🕐 ticket office and Exposición de Trofeos Tues-Sun 10.30am-7.30pm (closed 2hrs before kick-off on match days)
- ⑤ Exposición de Trofeos adult/concession €3.50/2.50
- ✗ see Chamberí pp75-6

That other place of worship – the stadium

DON'T MISS
- a look at the green, green grass of Real Madrid's pitch
- squatting down and having your pic taken in front of a life-size photo of the team

PLAZA DE LA CIBELES   (3, E14)

At the intersection of Paseo del Prado and Calle de Alcalá, this glorious fountain is one of Madrid's most enduring symbols and recognisable monuments. The fountain at the centre of this busy junction depicts the Ancient Greek goddess of nature, Cybele, in a chariot drawn by two lions. The story behind this myth is as follows: Cybele had Atalanta and Hippomenes (a match made by none other than Aphrodite herself) turned into lions and shackled to her chariot for having profaned her temple. Aphrodite had tricked them into this, due to her displeasure at the couple's apparent ingratitude for her good work.

INFORMATION

Ⓜ Banco de España
✕ see Chueca pp76-7 or Salamanca & Retiro pp85-6

The fountain was erected in 1780 by Ventura Rodríguez and José Hermosilla. As befits a monumental fountain, it is surrounded by some appropriately monumental architecture: the 1904 Palacio de Comunicaciones (see p44), the 1873 Palacio de Linares, the 18th-century Palacio Buenavista and the 19th-century Banco de España.

King Carlos III thought the fountain was so beautiful that he wanted to have it moved to the gardens of the Granja de San Ildefonso, on the road to Segovia, but this idea did not meet with the approval of locals. On the eve of big Real Madrid matches, the fountain is boarded up in an effort to protect it from idiotic fans (see boxed text).

Lapping it up

When Real Madrid wins a big match, the club's supporters like to commandeer the fountain for their festivities. The entire plaza and surrounding streets can get *packed* with revellers, and the damage to the fountain and litter left behind is not a pretty sight.

Giddy up – Plaza de la Cibeles

IGLESIA-CATEDRAL DE SAN ISIDRO (LA COLEGIATA)

(3, J8)

1767 was not a good year for the Jesuit order, as it was the year when King Carlos III had them expelled from Spain. This meant that this austere,

INFORMATION

- ✉ Calle de Toledo 37
- ☎ 91 369 20 37
- Ⓜ La Latina or Tirso de Molina
- ⊙ 8am-noon & 6-8.30pm
- ✗ see La Latina to Lavapiés pp81-2

sturdy-looking baroque basilica (designed by Pedro Sánchez) underwent a few changes from its status as Colegio Imperial (from which it gets it nickname, La Colegiata). Originally built in the 1620s, Carlos III decided that Ventura Rodríguez should remodel the interior, and an elaborate job was done, with a lavish altar drawing the attention of visitors.

The building's name was also changed to Catedral de San Isidro, after Madrid's patron saint. His remains were moved here in 1769 (in the third chapel to the left from the entrance) after resting in the Iglesia de San Andrés (see p40). He's been taken out of the basilica twice (1896 and 1947) to encourage the heavens to open up and rain. No matter what the weather is like, it's pretty unlikely that such an event will take place when you're visiting Madrid!

During the reign of King Fernando VII (1814–33), the basilica was returned to the Jesuit order, and from 1885 until 1993 it served as Madrid's 'temporary' cathedral, while the construction of the Catedral de Nuestra Señora de la Almudena (see p39) was carried out.

Iglesia-Catedral de San Isidro

A Leading School

Jesuit schools have a reputation for academic and moral rigour. It's no surprise then to learn that the **Instituto de San Isidro**, next door to Iglesia-Catedral de San Isidro, was the place where many of Spain's leading figures were educated from the 16th century onwards. You can wander in and look at the elegant courtyard, although the rest remains closed.

CASA DE CAMPO   (3, E1)

Casa de Campo is a huge expanse of scrubland spreading west of the Río Manzanares for 1740 hectares. This semi-wilderness was in royal hunting hands until 1931, after which the second republic made it accessible to the public. It's certainly not as attractive as the Parque del Buen Retiro, but it is effective as a mini-getaway for those who are finding Madrid a little congested, and there is plenty on offer.

INFORMATION

☎ 91 463 63 34
Ⓜ Batán, Lago or Norte

During the civil war, many of Franco's troops used the area to shell Madrid, and trenches are still scattered about the park. You can enter at the metro stop Lago or by air with the Teleférico de Rosales (see p46), and indulge in a little R&R, thanks to Casa de Campo's swimming pools, tennis courts and lake (see pp49–50). The park is also a popular spot for cyclists and joggers, and er, other types (see boxed text).

For the littlies, there's the **Parque de Atracciones** (see p47). It's also a popular past-time to hang out with a coffee or linger over lunch at some of the *terrazas* (outdoor cafés) that skirt the lake's edge. If you enter via the Batán metro stop, you'll be close to Madrid's zoo and aquarium (see p48). This stop is also close to the Andalucian-style ranch (known as Batán) that houses the bulls des-

Ladies of the Night (and Day)

Day or night, parts of Casa de Campo can seem a little more clogged with traffic than they should be. If you enter the park during the day, you'll notice that a lot of the winding roads are crawling with cars steered by solo men. And that a lot of scantily clad women seem to be just hanging around. During the evening, business really hots up, with prostitutes and punters jockeying for position around the lake. If you're taking the kids here, maybe it's best to do so during the day.

tined to go crazy at a red rag – China shop-style – in the bloody spectacle known as the Fiestas de San Isidro (see p89).

Casa de Campo from the teleférico

MUSEO SOROLLA   (4, G7)

Built in 1910, the former home of Valencian artist Joaquín Sorolla is a must-see. Left largely as it was in 1923 (the year of his death), the stunning house now holds an impressive collection of his light-filled impressionist works, plus articles and collections (tiles and ceramics) acquired by the artist during his lifetime. The ground floor gives a great idea of the manner in which Sorolla lived and worked, with a sun-drenched studio (courtesy of some judiciously placed skylights) and a neat little spot for him to take a nap on a Turkish bed. This is also the area where his various collections are displayed.

INFORMATION

- ✉ Paseo del General Martínez Campos 37
- ☎ 91 310 15 84
- ⓔ www.mcu.es/ nmuseos/sorolla/ index.html
- Ⓜ Rubén Darío or Iglesia
- ⊘ Tues-Sat 10am-3pm, Sun 10am-2pm
- Ⓢ adult/concession €2.40/1.20, free under-18 & over-65

The first floor (the former sleeping quarters) takes you to the gallery that houses works from the 1890s onwards. Sorolla's work is dominated by an easy-on-the-eye style of portraiture and landscape. You won't need to whip out your dictionary of art theory to decipher these attractive scenes of pretty ladies at rest or various Spaniards at their leisure or toil. However, the art is arranged chronologically, which makes Sorolla's earlier works easily recognisable for their dark tones. They're especially dark for someone who was renowned for his mastery of depicting light.

There's a heavenly Moorish-style garden on the grounds too, which was designed by the artist himself. Spending some time here will make you forget that you're in one of Europe's most frantic cities.

The must-see Museo Sorolla

Better Than Ever

Behind closed doors, the museum has recently been spruced up. It was in fact closed at the time of research, but should be ready and raring to go by the time you read this, so go!

sights & activities

NEIGHBOURHOODS

South of Gran Vía and west of Paseo de la Castellana is the area that will take most of your attention. West of the Palacio Real lies the **Los Austrias** *barrio* (neighbourhood), sometimes called the *morería*, or Moorish quarter, with charming narrow streets and traditional restaurants.

West of this, from Calle de Toledo, are the **La Latina** and **Lavapiés** *barrios*, which are rich examples of *castizo* (distinctly Madrid) life mixed with new waves of immigration.

Huertas and **Santa Ana** are *the* eating and drinking zones, with thousands of bars and big crowds at night. It was also the scene of the literary golden age in the 17th century.

North of Gran Vía lies the pink barrio of **Chueca**, a respectable 19th-century area that fell on hard times and has been rejuvenated by the gay community. West of this is **Malasaña**, a working-class district popular for nightlife, with a bohemian feel. Further west, you'll find **Argüelles**, with pleasant *terrazas* (outdoor cafés) and a distinctly untouristed feel. North of Malasaña is the area known as **Chamberí**, which underwent development in the second half of the 19th century but still retains a *castizo* air and a family atmosphere, despite not being in the oldest part of the city.

Off the Beaten Track

The areas that feel most touristy in Madrid tend to surround Plaza de la Puerta del Sol and Plaza Mayor, or the 'big three' art museums. For the most part, La Latina, Lavapiés, Chueca and Malasaña remain faithfully local haunts, except at night, when Madrid becomes a mobile party town. The city's parks are also good places to escape to during the week.

East of Paseo de la Castellana is the stylish **Salamanca** *ensanche* (extension), constructed on a grid during the late 19th century. Its tree-lined streets play host to some of the fanciest shops in Madrid. South of this, bordering the Parque del Buen Retiro, the **Retiro** neighbourhood feels less exclusive but is still pleasant, thanks to its greenery.

View from El Viajero Terrace (p91)

MUSEUMS & GALLERIES

Biblioteca Nacional & Museo del Libro
(3, C15) The Biblioteca Nacional was commissioned in 1865 by Isabel II and completed in 1892. Inside you'll find some cleverly arranged collections on the history of writing and the gathering of knowledge. The *museo* is bibliophile heaven – with Arabic texts, illuminated manuscripts, and centuries-old Torahs.
✉ **Paseo de Recoletos 20, Salamanca** ☎ **91 580 78 00** e www .bne.es Ⓜ **Colón** ⏰ **Biblioteca Mon-Fri 9am-9pm, Sat 9am-2pm; museo Tues-Sat 10am-9pm, Sun 10am-2pm** ⑤ **free** ♿ **good**

Casa de la Moneda
(2, L9) Numismatic maniacs can revel in coins from throughout the ages at this slightly down-at-heel museum in the National Mint. It runs the gamut from Ancient Greek coins to the poor old peseta, which was relegated in 2002 to the fiscal dustbin.
✉ **Calle del Doctor Esquerdo 36, Retiro** ☎ **91 566 65 44** Ⓜ **O'Donnell** ⏰ **Tues-Fri 10am-2.30pm & 5-7.30pm, Sat, Sun & hols 10am-2.30pm** ⑤ **free**

Casa de Lope de Vega
(3, H12) Felix Lope de Vega was one of Spain's leading golden-age writers, and he moved to this austere-looking house in 1610, remaining here until his death in 1635. You wouldn't really know he's no longer with us though, as it's filled with memorabilia pertaining to his life and times, giving a wonderful insight into life in Madrid in the 17th century.
✉ **Calle de Cervantes 11, Huertas** ☎ **91 429 92 16** Ⓜ **Antón Martín** ⏰ **Tues-Fri 9.30am-2pm, Sat 10am-noon** ⑤ **adult/concession €1.50/90c**

Ermita de San Antonio de la Florida
(2, K1) This small hermitage has two small chapels: the southern one contains a magnificent dome fresco by Goya depicting the miracle of St Anthony. The crowd of people swarming around the saint are interesting not just for Goya's extraordinary skills, but also because they've been placed in the dome, an area usually reserved for heavenly subjects.
✉ **Glorieta de la Florida 5, Argüelles** ☎ **91 542 07 22** e **www.munimadrid .es/ermita** Ⓜ **Príncipe Pío** ⏰ **Tues-Fri 10am-2pm & 4-8pm, Sat & Sun 10am-2pm, closed hols** ⑤ **adult/concession €1.80/90c, free Wed & Sun**

Museo de San Isidro p37

Fundación Juan March
(4, J11) Businessman Juan March established this cultural and scientific foundation in 1955, and the modern facilities house a permanent collection of contemporary Spanish art, including some way-out sculptures on its grounds. Temporary exhibitions and concerts are also held here on a regular basis (see also p96).
✉ **Calle de Castelló 77, Salamanca** ☎ **91 435 42 40** e **www.march.es** Ⓜ **Núñez de Balboa** ⏰ **Mon-Sat 10am-2pm & 5.30-9pm, Sat, Sun &**

Faeces in the Crowd
Madrid can be a tricky town to negotiate in minimalist footwear, such as strappy sandals or slides. Why? No-one seems remotely interested in cleaning up their dog's poo. And Madrid's dogs poo freely and frequently. Yep, the streets get a good regular hosing, but you'll always have to remember to keep an eye on where you're treading.

hols 10am-2pm ⑤ free ⅙ good

Museo de América
(2, H1) When the Spaniards weren't loading their ships with Latin American gold, they found a bit of room for transporting ceramics, statuary, jewellery, hunting implements and a few shrunken heads from indigenous cultures. Some good temporary exhibitions with Latin American themes are also held in this interesting museum.
✉ Avenida de los Reyes Católicos 6, Moncloa ☎ 91 549 26 41 Ⓜ Moncloa ⏰ Tues-Sat 10am-3pm, Sun & hols 10am-2pm ⑤ adult/concession €3/1.50

Museo Arqueológico Nacional **(3, C15)**
Founded by royal decree in 1867, this is one mother of a royal collection, with goodies from prehistory to Ancient Egypt, Greece and Rome, up to Mudéjar Spain. Among other things, keep an eye out for the sarcophagus of Amemenhat (Room 13), the Lady of Elche (Room 20), Livia (Room 21), Recesvinio's crown (Room 29) and the Aljafería arch (Room 30).
✉ Calle Serrano 13, Salamanca ☎ 91 577 79 12 e www.man.es Ⓜ Serrano or Colón ☎ Recoletos ⏰ Tues-Sat 9.30am-8.30pm, Sun 9.30am-2.30pm, closed Mon & hols ⑤ adult/concession €3/1.50; free under-18, over-65, Sat 2.30-8.30pm & Sun 9.30am-2.30pm ⅙ good

Museo de Cerralbo
(3, C5) This is the former 19th-century home of the 17th Marqués de Cerralbo – politician, poet, archaeologist, as well as avid collector. The collection has been kept close to how the Marqués lived, and according to his wishes. It includes religious paintings (El Greco's *Éxtasis de San Francisco* is stunning), clocks, suits of armour, jewellery and books. Most of the opulent rooms are fascinating – you'll feel like a right sticky-beak at times.
✉ Calle de Ventura Rodríguez 17, Argüelles ☎ 91 547 36 46 Ⓜ Plaza de España or Ventura Rodríguez ⏰ Tues-Sat 9.30am-2.30pm, Sun 10am-2pm ⑤ adult/concession €2.40/1.20; free under-18, over-65, Wed & Sun

Museo del Ejército
(3, G15) This army museum is housed in what was the Salón de Reinos del Buen Retiro in one of the few remaining parts of the Palacio del Buen Retiro. There's a room devoted to the nationalist campaign in the civil war and the Sala Árabe room contains the sword of Boabdil – who was the last Muslim ruler of Granada. Apparently this museum is going to be shifted to the alcázar in Toledo (see p56), but we didn't see any signs of movement at the time of research.
✉ Calle de Méndez Núñez 1, Retiro ☎ 91 522 89 77 Ⓜ Banco de España ⏰ Tues-Sat 10am-2pm ⑤ adult/ concession 60c/30c, free seniors & Sat

Museo de San Isidro
(3, J6) Madrid's patron saint has a tastefully renovated museum named after him, where you can see various archaeological finds from old Madrid, including mosaic fragments from the Roman villa in Carabanchel (now a southern suburb). The building also has a 16th-century courtyard, a 17th-century chapel and some very interesting displays based on the history of Madrid.
✉ Plaza de San Andrés 2, Los Austrias ☎ 91 366 74 15 e www.munimadrid.es/museosanisidro Ⓜ La Latina or Tirso de Molina ☎ 3, 17, 18, 23, 35, 60 ⏰ Tues-Fri 9.30am-8pm, Sat & Sun 10am-2pm ⑤ free ⅙ good

Baroque doorway, Museo Municipal de Madrid p38

Museo Lázaro Galdiano **(4, G9)**
A rich collection of delightful works by artists such as Van Eyck, Bosch, Zurbarán, Ribera, Goya, Gainsborough and Constable are held here, with ceilings painted according to the

Real Academia de Bellas Artes de San Fernando

room's particular function. It was closed in 2002 for renovations.
✉ Calle de Serrano 122, Salamanca ☎ 91 561 60 84 @ www.flg.es Ⓜ Rubén Darío or Gregorio Marañón Ⓢ free

Museo Municipal de Madrid (3, B11)
A restored baroque entrance greets visitors to this museum, but unfortunately, that's all we got to see – restoration works should be finished by the time you read this, with some interesting maps and manuscripts on display. The building was founded in 1673 and retains its original chapel and some decent

paintings, which are also worth seeing.
✉ Calle de Fuencarral 78, Chueca ☎ 91 588 86 72 @ smuseosm @munimadrid.es Ⓜ Tribunal ⏱ Tues-Fri 9.30am-8pm, Sat & Sun 10am-2pm Ⓢ adult/concession €1.80/90c ♿ good

Museo Nacional de Artes Decorativas
(3, F15) Spread over five floors, this museum presents a fascinating collection of glassware, ceramics, furniture, fabrics and utensils in an attractive setting, plus some well reconstructed rooms. Our favourite was the *alcoba*, a room used for 'conjugal unions'. But we also loved the parquetry

floors and the detailed ceilings – and the fifth floor's tiled 18th-century kitchen.
✉ Calle de Montalbán 12, Retiro ☎ 91 532 64 99 Ⓜ Banco de España ⏱ Tues-Sat 9.30am-2pm, Sun 10am-2pm Ⓢ adult/concession €2.40/1.20; free under-18, over-65 & Sun

Museo Romántico
(3, B11) A minor treasure trove of mostly 19th-century paintings, furniture and porcelain. The downstairs rooms contain a variety of books, photographs and documents relating to the life of the Marqués de la Vega-Inclán, while his personal collection is upstairs. It's an interesting insight into what upper-class houses were like in the 19th century. The *museo* was closed for renovation when we visited, so check.
✉ Calle de San Mateo 13, Chueca ☎ 91 448 10 45 Ⓜ Tribunal ⏱ Tues-Fri 9am-3pm, Sat, Sun & hols 10am-2pm Ⓢ free

Real Academia de Bellas Artes de San Fernando (3, F11)
This was founded by King Fernando VI in the 18th century as a centre to train artists; this rather fusty gallery can boast that both Picasso and Dalí studied here. Spanish artists of note displayed include José de Ribera, El Greco, Bravo Murillo, Goya and Sorolla.
✉ Calle de Alcalá 13, Sol & Gran Vía ☎ 91 524 08 64 Ⓜ Sevilla ⏱ Tues-Fri 9am-7pm, Sat-Mon 9am-2.30pm Ⓢ adult/concession €2.40/1.20

CHURCHES & CATHEDRALS

Basílica de San Miguel (3, H7)
This basilica stands on the site of an earlier Romanesque church. The present edifice was built between 1739 and 1745 and is an interesting example of late baroque. The interior (no photos allowed) is a mix of rococo and the contemporary.
✉ Calle de San Justo 4, Los Austrias ☎ 91 548 40 11 Ⓜ Ópera or La Latina ◷ Mon-Sat 11am-12.15pm & 5.30-7pm Ⓢ free

Catedral de Nuestra Señora de la Almudena

Capilla del Obispo
(3, J6) This chapel is a rare example of the transitional style from Gothic to Renaissance. Built to house San Isidro's remains (which are no longer here) by the Vargas family, it's a tricky proposition to get inside. You'll probably have to ask at a tourist office if a temporary exhibition is on.
✉ Plaza de la Paja, Los Austrias Ⓜ La Latina Ⓢ free

Catedral de Nuestra Señora de la Almudena (3, G5)
Just south of the Palacio Real, Madrid's cathedral is externally grand and internally bland. It was finally completed in 1993 after a good 110 years of construction – the Spanish civil war was a major interruption. The present place of worship may well be a new building, but this site (and the areas nearby) have served a religious purpose in one way or another since the city's earliest settlement.
✉ Calle de Bailén, Los Austrias ☎ 91 542 22 00 ℮ www.patrimonio nacional.es Ⓜ Ópera ◷ Sep-Jun 9am-9pm; Jul & Aug 10am-2pm & 5-9pm Ⓢ free ♿ good

Iglesia de San Ginés
(3, F8) One of Madrid's oldest churches, San Ginés has been here in some shape or form since the 14th century. There's also speculation that pre-1085, when Christians arrived in Madrid, a Mozarabic community (Christians in Muslim territory) had its parish church on the site. The dark interior is ideal for contemplation of matters both spiritual and artistic (note the El Greco painting).
✉ Calle de San Martín, Los Austrias Ⓜ Ópera or Sol ◷ 8.45am-1pm & 6-9 pm Ⓢ free

Doorway detail, Iglesia de San Jerónimo el Real p40

Iglesia de San Andrés (3, J6)

San Andrés suffered severe damage during the civil war, but its exterior looks as neat and shiny as a new pin now. The interior features some baroque decorative touches and a lovely dome, with plump cherubs running riot in a sea of colour.

✉ **Plaza de San Andrés, Los Austrias** Ⓜ **La Latina** ⏱ **9am-1pm & 6-8pm** Ⓢ **free**

Blink and You'd Miss It ...

You could easily be forgiven for failing to notice the small brick structure on the corner of Calle de Fuencarral and Calle de Augusto Figueroa in Chueca (3, C11). It's Madrid's tiniest church, and has little more than a crucifix and diminutive altar.

Iglesia de San Jerónimo el Real

(3, H15) This church was constructed in the 16th century and was once the nucleus of the extremely powerful Hieronymite monastery. The interior structure is a 19th century remodelling that gives more than a nod to the Monasterio de San Juan de los Reyes in Toledo. King Alfonso XIII was married here in 1906, and King Juan Carlos I was crowned here in 1975.

✉ **Calle del Moreto 4, Retiro** ☎ **91 421 35 78** Ⓜ **Banco de España** ⏱ **9am-1.30pm & 6-8pm** Ⓢ **free** ♿ **good**

Iglesia de San Nicolás de los Servitas (3, G6)

A few periods are represented in this church (which is considered the oldest surviving church in the city), from the 12th-century Mudéjar bell tower, to the church itself, which dates in part from the 15th century – note the late-Gothic interior vaulting and timber ceiling. There are 18th-century baroque touches too.

✉ **Plaza de San Nicolás, Los Austrias** ☎ **91 559 40 64** Ⓜ **Ópera** ⏱ **Mon 8.30am-2pm, Tues-Sat 8.30-9.30am & 6.30-8.30pm, Sun 10am-2pm & 6.30-8.30pm** Ⓢ **free**

Iglesia de San Pedro El Viejo (3, J6)

Those wanting to see one of the few remaining examples of Mudéjar architecture should raise their eyes to San Pedro's bell tower, which dates from the 14th century.

✉ **Costanilla de San Pedro, Los Austrias** ☎ **91 365 12 84** Ⓜ **La Latina** Ⓢ **free**

Iglesia de Santa Bárbara (3, C14)

This large baroque church was built between 1750 and 1757 for Bárbara de Braganza, the wife of Fernando VI. External design was left in the capable hands of François Carlier, while the splendid interior was the work of Doménico Olivieri. It features a painting by Corrado Giaquinto and is also the final resting place of Fernando VI himself.

✉ **Calle del General Castaños 2, Chueca**

Ⓜ **Alonso Martínez or Colón** ⏱ **Mon-Fri 9am-1pm & 5-9pm, Sun & hols 10am-1pm & 5-9pm** Ⓢ **free**

Oratorio de Caballero de Gracia

(3, E11) This charming oratory was designed in the neoclassical style by Juan de Villanueva in 1795 and declared a national monument in 1956. The interior features some fine paintings and a stunning altar.

✉ **Calle Caballero de Gracia 5, Gran Vía** Ⓜ **Gran Vía or Sevilla** ⏱ **unreliable, check with tourist office** Ⓢ **free**

Real Monasterio de la Encarnación (3, E6)

This enclosed Augustine convent has some decent royal portraiture (it was founded by Felipe III and Margarita of Austria in 1611). However, the real reason for visiting is the jam-packed *reliquiario*, which has over 700 assorted skulls and bones, bits of the True Cross and a vial of St Pantaleón's blood – which liquefies on the night of 26 July.

✉ **Plaza de la Encarnación, Sol & Gran Vía** ☎ **91 454 88 00** 📧 **www.patrimonio nacional.es** Ⓜ **Ópera** ⏱ **Tues-Thur & Sat 10.30am-12.45pm & 4-5.45pm, Fri 10.30am-12.45pm, Sun & hols 11am-1.45pm** Ⓢ **adult/concession €3.45/1.80 (free under-5 & Wed for EU citizens), combined ticket (valid 7 days) with Real Monasterio de las Descalzas Reales (see p22) €6/3.30**

PLAZAS & PARKS

Parque del Oeste
(2, J1) Nestled between the university and Moncloa metro station, this large park is a surprisingly tranquil and beautiful place to get some green in Madrid. The park is the site of the deaths of many locals at the hands of Napoleon's army in 1808, and in recent times an on-off 'beat' for transexual prostitutes and their customers at night.
Ⓜ Moncloa

Big on Botero
Plaza de Colón's most attractive artwork is the sculpture by Fernando Botero of *Man on a Mule*. Also look out for his delightfully cheeky *Reclining Woman* on Paseo de la Castellana.

Plaza de Chueca
(3, C12) This party-loving plaza is named after a composer of *zarzuelas* (light opera) and is at its best late at night. Locals, gays, party types and anyone else hangs out at the tables, benches and chairs and on the ground. It's flanked by Calle de Gravina, Calle de Augusto Figueroa, apartments and more than a few banners protesting about the racket.
Ⓜ Chueca

Plaza de Colón
(3, B15) As an inspired memorial to Christopher Columbus and his discovery of America, this plaza makes a great transport hub. The *Monumento a Colón* (statue of Colombus) ain't too bad, but the big slab known as the *Monumento al Descubrimiento* (Monument to the Discovery) has a distinctly 1970s cobbled-together feel about it. Still, there's a cultural centre (Centro Cultural de la Villa) underneath it all (see p96), which offers lots of entertainment potential.
Ⓜ Colón or Serrano

Plaza de España
(3, C6) Not as grand as you'd think, given its name, but this plaza is a popular meeting spot for plenty of *madrileños* and has some welcoming seats under trees for hot days. Its north side faces the bombastic Edificio de España, but its centre has a charming bronze statue of Miguel de Cervantes, with his famous characters Don Quixote and Sancho Panza at his feet.
Ⓜ Plaza de España
♿ good

Plaza de la Paja
(3, J6) This plaza's name translates to Straw Square, and it was once the hub of Madrid in medieval times. It's been lovingly restored over the years, and affords some attractive views of surrounding buildings.
Ⓜ La Latina

Plaza de Neptuno
(3, H14) Officially known as Plaza de Cánovas del Castillo, but more readily referred to as 'the roundabout with Neptune near the Prado'. The sculpture of the sea-god is, for the record, by Juan Pascal de Mena. Atlético Madrid fans flock here when their team is victorious, halting traffic.
Ⓜ Banco de España

Neptune, Plaza de Neptuno

Plaza de Olivade
(4, H4) You won't find anything of historical interest here but we think it's one of the city's most pleasant afternoon/evening spots. There's a large open area, plenty of small bars with outdoor seating, some pretty rose bushes and an authentically local feel, with few tourists disturbing the social intercourse.
Ⓜ Bilbao, Quevado or Iglesia

Plaza de Oriente
(3, F6) Between the Palacio Real and the Teatro Real is one of Madrid's loveliest plazas, which gets its French feel from Joseph Bonaparte's rule in the early 1800s. It contains an equestrian statue of Felipe IV and statues of ancient monarchs that were supposed to adorn the Palacio Real but were deemed too heavy.
Ⓜ Ópera ♿ good

Plaza de San Andrés to Plaza de la Cebada (3, K6)

This area is a conglomeration of tiny plazas that comprise one of Madrid's most pleasant spots to unwind. Plaza de San Andrés sports the church of the same name and some nice community murals. Other mini-plazas flanking it are plazas de los Carros, de Puerta de Moros and del Humiladero. Plaza de la Cebada has a market and some of the best nighttime terraces in Madrid.

Ⓜ La Latina

Plaza de Santa Ana

(3, H11) You can thank Joseph Bonaparte for this square, as he demolished the 16th-century Convent of Santa Ana to make room for its construction. A long-famous drinking haunt, it's been tarted up recently and many feel it has lost its earthy charm and now has an antiseptic feel. Still, it's buzzing every afternoon and night of the week, and there's even play equipment for the kids (see boxed text below).

Ⓜ Sevilla or Antón Martín ⓰ good

Lorca statue, Plaza de Santa Ana

Plaza del Callao

(3, E9) On Sundays madrileños like to go to the movies, and this plaza (at the intersection of Gran Vía and Calle de Preciados) is where the hordes come. There are seven cinemas here (films are dubbed into Spanish if they're foreign), with some eye-catchingly garish advertising billboards and banners, giving the place a lively feel.

Ⓜ Callao

Plaza del Dos de Mayo (3, A9)

This square gets its name from the heroic last stand that madrileños took against Napoleon's troops on 2 May 1808. All that's left of the barracks that were here at the time is an arch. In more recent times, the plaza has had a reputation as the party spot for underage drinkers, although recent legislation has curbed the booze-and-hormone explosion.

Ⓜ Noviciado or Tribunal

Plaza de Santo Domingo (3, E7)

Named after a huge Dominican monastery that once stood here, this plaza's missing namesake is a telling indication of the power of anticlericalism in 19th-century Spain. There's not much to see though.

Ⓜ Santo Domingo

Plaza de la Puerta del Sol (3, G9)

This is Madrid's most central point and the psychological centre of town. Check out the small plaque on the southern side that marks km 0, the point from which distances are measured along the country's highways. A good meeting point is the bronze statue of a bear nuzzling a *madroño* (strawberry tree).

Ⓜ Sol

Playtime

Madrid tries not to forget the civic needs of even its tiniest citizens by including play equipment in some of its plazas. You can check out Plaza de Santa Ana or the more restrained Plaza de Olivade in Chamberí (among others) for slides and other kiddies' things.

Hangin' with the Play Set

NOTABLE BUILDINGS & MONUMENTS

Azca (4, B8)
This development goes by the nickname 'Little Manhattan', and construction started in the late 1960s. The 1980s saw it come into its own though as the epicentre of yuppie life, with big corporations, shops, restaurants and plenty of glass, concrete and steel. The most notable features of the complex are the Torres Puerta Europa and Picasso skyscrapers, designed by Miguel Oriol e Ybarra (1982) and Minoru Yamasaki (1989), respectively.
✉ Paseo de la Castellana 95, Coplejo Azca Ⓜ Lima or Nuevos Ministerios
♿ good

Edificio de España
(3, C6) For some strange reason, this building, which towers over Plaza de España, is not as hideous as you'd expect fascist-era architecture to be. The building was constructed between 1947 and 1953 when Spain was not on friendly terms with the rest of the world. Needless to say, it became a symbol of the 'we don't need them' school of thought for the Franco era. It looks best at sunset.
✉ Plaza de España, Sol & Gran Vía Ⓜ Plaza de España

Edificio Grassy
(3, E12) Look for the Piaget sign to identify this, one of Gran Vía's most elegant buildings. It was built in 1916 (Spain had money for such things thanks to her neutrality in WWI) and has a circular 'temple' as

its crown. Given the presence of the Piaget sign, it's only fitting that there's a museum of timepieces in the basement.
✉ Gran Vía 1, Gran Vía ☎ 91 532 10 07 Ⓜ Banco de España ⏰ museum Mon-Sat 10am-1pm & 5-8pm

Edificio Metropolis

Edificio Metropolis
(3, F12) You could be forgiven for thinking you're in Paris when you catch sight of this magnificent building. It was designed by Jules and Raymond Février and was completed in 1910 (although the victory statue was only placed on top in 1975). Note the four

allegorical sculptures that represent Agriculture, Commerce, Mining and Industry, and the beautiful dome with gilded details.
✉ Calle de Alcalá 39, Gran Vía Ⓜ Banco de España or Sevilla

Faro de Madrid
(2, H1) It may look like an air traffic control tower, but the *faro* (literally, 'lighthouse') exists just to provide a panoramic view of Madrid from 92m up. The views *are* good, though the tower's lacking in the usual touristy facilities (no café or restaurant). Look southeast towards the city centre and you'll see the Arco de la Victoria – the archway built to celebrate Franco's victory in the civil war.
✉ Avenida de los Reyes Catolicos, Moncloa ☎ 91 544 81 04 Ⓜ Moncloa ⏰ Tues-Sun 10am-2pm & 5-9pm 💲 adult/concession €1/50c

La Corrala (2, O4)
Yep, it's a tenement block, but it's not going to scare you. La Corrala is a great example of 19th-century timber-framed apartment

In-your-face edifice: Edificio de España

complexes that were constructed in Madrid. It was declared a historic monument in 1977, and has been restored (though it still has an unfinished feel about it), enabling it to be used as a backdrop for summertime performances.
✉ **Calle de Mesón de Paredes 65, Lavapiés** Ⓜ **Lavapiés**

Muralla Árabe
(3, H5) This is a fragment of the city wall built by Madrid's early medieval Muslim rulers. The earliest sections date from the 9th century, while others date from the 12th and 13th centuries. The council organises open-air theatre and music performances here during summer.
✉ **Cuesta de la Vega, Los Austrias** Ⓜ **Ópera**

Palacio de Comunicaciones
(3, E14) This must be one of the most elaborate post offices in the world, and the word 'palace' is not misplaced. Some find it much too grandiose, while others enjoy the sense of occasion that comes with buying a stamp. It was built in 1904 by Antonio Palacios Ramilo, in the North American monumental style, and has Gothic and Renaissance touches.
✉ **Plaza de la Cibeles**
☎ **91 396 26 79**

Ⓜ **Banco de España**
🕙 **Mon-Fri 8.30am-9.30pm, Sat 8.30am-2pm**

Palacio de Liria
(3, A6) This fabulous 1780 palace is home to works by masters including Titian, Rembrandt, Rubens, Goya and El Greco, but there's a slight catch: it's still owned by a duchess, and to get a peek inside you'll need to apply in writing to: Don Miguel, Calle de Princesa 20, 28008 Madrid, to request a visit (which is possible Fri 11am & noon). Then you'll have a *long* wait (of at least six months). It's just as well that the view from the

The monumental Plaza de Toros Monumental de las Ventas p45

grounds' gates is so impressive.

✉ **Calle de Princesa 20, Malasaña**
☎ **91 547 53 02**
Ⓜ **Ventura Rodríguez**

Plaza de Toros Monumental de Las Ventas (2, J10)
This is the biggest and most important bullring in the world, and it's suitably impressive in appearance. Built in 1929 in the neo-Mudéjar style and featuring some lovely tilework, it has the capacity to hold over 20,000 spectators. It's worth a visit, even if you're not seeing a bullfight.
✉ **Calle de Alcalá 237, Las Ventas**
☎ **91 356 22 00**
ⓔ **www.las-ventas.com**
Ⓜ **Las Ventas**

Puente de Segovia (3, H1)
This fine nine-arched stone bridge was constructed in 1584 by Juan de Herrera for Felipe II, as a means of making San Lorenzo de El Escorial (see p55) more accessible. It runs from Calle de Segovia, heading west, and is worth crossing, though the river beneath (Río Manzanares) isn't much chop.
Ⓜ **Puerta del Ángel**
♿ **good**

Sala del Canal de Isabel II (4, E4)
This 1911 water tower was built in the neo-Mudéjar style, and ceased active water service in 1952. However, photographic exhibitions are sometimes held here, so it's worth checking listings and making the trip.
✉ **Calle de Santa Engracia 125, Vallehermoso** ☎ **91**

445 10 00 Ⓜ **Rios Rosas** ⏰ **Tues-Sat 10am-2pm & 5-9pm, Sun & hols 10am-2pm** ⑤ **free** ♿ **good**

Sociedad General de Autores y Editores (3, B12)
You'll have to admire this modernist architectural confection from the outside, which is no trouble, as it resembles a half-melted ice cream cake and is hard to miss. It was designed by José Grasés Riera in 1902 for the banker Javier González Longoria. Now it's the home of Madrid's book nerds' society.
✉ **cnr Calle de Pelayo & Calle de Fernando VI, Chueca** ☎ **91 349 95 14** Ⓜ **Alonso Martínez**

Teatro Real (3, F6)
Re-opened in 1987 and an opulent mix of state-of-the-art theatre technology and Palacio Real-style grandeur (although some sections are reminiscent of imposing-but-insipid big hotels), a tour of the Teatro Real is nifty for those who want a peek inside without seeing a performance. There are guided tours (in Spanish, approximately 1hr).
✉ **Plaza de Oriente, Los Austrias** ☎ **91 5 16 06 96** ⓔ **www .teatro-real.com** Ⓜ **Ópera** ⏰ **guided tours Tues-Sun 10.30am-1.30pm** ⑤ **€3/1.80, free under-7** ♿ **good**

Telefónica (3, E10)
This colossus was constructed in the 1920s with the formation of the national phone company. Designed by US architect

Louis S Weeks, it was the tallest building in the city for years. During the civil war, its prominence made it a constant target for nationalist artillery.
✉ **Gran Via 28, Gran Via** ☎ **91 522 66 45** Ⓜ **Gran Vía** ♿ **good**

Templo de Debod (3, C3)
The Templo de Debod is something of an attention-catcher, not only for its prime position in the Parque de la Montaña, but also for the fact that it's a 2200 year-old Egyptian temple, gratefully transported to Spain in 1968 as a gesture of Egyptian thanks for Spain's help in building the Aswan High Dam.
✉ **Paseo del Pintor Rosales, Argüelles**
☎ **91 366 74 15**
Ⓜ **Plaza de España**
⏰ **1 Apr-30 Sep Tues-Fri 10am-2pm & 6-8pm, Sat & Sun 10am-2pm; 1 Oct-31 Mar Tues-Fri 9.45am-1.45pm & 4.15-6.15pm, Sat & Sun 10am-2pm** ⑤ **adult/ concession €1.80/90c, free Wed & Sun** ♿ **good**

Torres Puerta Europa (2, C6)
The leaning Torres Puerta Europa are a remarkable addition to Paseo de la Castellana, mostly because they stand 115m high and have a 15-degree tilt. Designed by John Burgee to symbolise a gateway to Europe, they are probably the most impressive modern structures in Madrid. Film buffs will remember them from the closing scenes of *Abre Los Ojos*.
✉ **Plaza de Castilla, Chamartín** Ⓜ **Plaza de Castilla** ♿ **good**

QUIRKY MADRID

Chocolatería de San Ginés (3, G8)
You may not think that a shop specialising in *churros y chocolate* sounds very quirky, but just look at the opening hours. If you've been partying till the early hours of the morning, this place is a rite of passage.

✉ Pasadizo de San Ginés, Los Austrias
☎ 91 365 65 46
Ⓜ Ópera ⏰ 6pm-7am

Museo Erótico de Madrid (3, H9)
Madrid now has a sex museum, where you can peruse all manner of resolve-stiffening devices, images and a S&M room. It's probably not suitable for the kids though, unless you're trying to scare them.

✉ Calle del Doctor Cortezo 2, La Latina
☎ 91 369 39 71
Ⓜ Tirso de Molina ⏰ Tues-Sat 11am-2pm & 6-9pm, Sun & hols 11am-2pm & 5-9pm
💲 €5.10/3.90

Museo de Esculturas al Aire Libre (4, H9)
A space you might stumble upon and one that's often

ignored by residents of Madrid, this open-air museum lies under the bridge connecting Paseo de Eduardo Dato and Calle de Juan Bravo. There are sculptures from prominent 20th-century Spanish artists (including Miró, Sánchez and Chillida) that enliven a space that's normally little more than an eyesore in most cities.

✉ Paseo de la Castellana 41
☎ 91 588 86 72
ℯ www.munimadrid .es/museoairelibre
Ⓜ Rubén Darío ⏰ 24hrs 💲 free

Museo Naval (3, F14)
This *museo* is a sea-dog's paradise in landlocked Madrid, and boasts dazzlingly well-crafted models of ships that'll have you itching to get out the hobby glue. Also worth noting is the surprisingly accurate parchment map (dating from 1500) of the 'known world' (it wasn't flat!), and the beautiful reproduction of the *Sala del Patronato*.

✉ Paseo del Prado 5, Retiro ☎ 91 379 52 99
Ⓜ Banco de España

⏰ Tues-Sun 10.30am-1.30pm 💲 free

Museo Taurino (2, J10)
On the right-hand side of Las Ventas, this place is steeped in bull. It's small and modern, with displays (English- and Spanish-language) devoted to the art/sport of man fighting bull. You'll see busts and paintings of famous bullfighters, the bloody suit worn by Manolete when he was killed by 'Islero' in 1947 and six enormous bulls' heads mounted on the wall.

✉ Plaza de Toros Monumental de las Ventas, Las Ventas
☎ 91 725 18 57
Ⓜ Ventas ⏰ Mon-Sat 9.30am-2.30pm, bullfight days 10am-1pm 💲 free

Teleférico de Rosales (2, K1)
To put it bluntly, this cable car is no great shakes in the excitement stakes, but it is an interesting way to enter Madrid's Casa de Campo, plus you'll get to see from on high the baffling amount of traffic crawling along the park's roads. The reason? Prostitutes work in the area. It makes for Madrid's quirkiest traffic jam.

✉ cnr Paseo del Pintor Rosales & Calle del Marqués de Urquijo, Argüelles ☎ 91 541 74 50 ℯ www.teleferico .com Ⓜ Argüelles or Ventura Rodríguez
⏰ Mon-Fri 11am-3pm & 5-9pm; Sat, Sun & hols 11am-9.30pm
💲 one way/return €2.80/4

Get initiated at Chocolatería de San Ginés

MADRID FOR CHILDREN

There's plenty to keep the little ones occupied in Madrid, from performance artists and buskers in plazas, parks and streets to attractions specifically aimed at children. Locals certainly don't ascribe to the 'children
should be seen and not heard' philosophy, and you'll find kids taking part
in plenty of late-night dinners surrounded by grown-ups, without a whiff
of condescension or irritation. Look for the 👶 with individual reviews in
the Places to Eat, Entertainment and Places to Stay chapters for more
child-friendly options.

Museo de Cera
(3, B15) If spending your
time and money guffawing
at waxen representations
of the rich, famous and
infamous is your thing,
then this is your place.
Adults will need to use
their imagination for some
of the depictions, but kids
are quite happy to wax lyri-
cal about the pseudo
celebs and ride the Tren de
Terror.
✉ Paseo de Recoletos
41, Chueca ☎ 91 308
08 25 Ⓜ Colón
🕐 10am-8.30pm
⑤ full visit (museo,
Tren de Terror,
Simulador) adult/
concession €12/7;
museo only €9/5

Museo del Ferrocarril
(2, P6) About 500m
south of Atocha station,
you'll find around 30
pieces of rolling stock at
this train museum, housed
in the disused 1880s
Estación de Delicias. Adults
will enjoy the café in the
1930s dining car, and kids

will love everything, especially the chance to plead
for train-related toys from
the shop.
✉ Paseo de las
Delicias 61, Delicias
☎ 902 22 88 22
🅴 www.museodel
ferrocarril.org
Ⓜ Delicias 🕐 Tues-Sun
10am-3pm ⑤ adult/
concession €3.50/2,
free Sat ♿ good

Museo Nacional de
Ciencias Naturales
(4, E8) Kids and adults
alike will love this place!
Fascinating permanent and
temporary exhibitions cover
topics as cool as the history of the earth and all
natural sciences, plus kids'
programs on weekends.
✉ Calle de José
Abascal 2, Salamanca
☎ 91 411 13 28
🅴 www.museociencias
.com Ⓜ Gregorio
Marañón 🕐 Tues-Fri
10am-6pm, Sat 10am-
8pm, Sun & hols 10am-
2.30pm, ⑤ adult/
concession €3/2.40

Parque Biológico
(1, E4) The 'Biological
Park' is a recent arrival on
Madrid's scene of animal
distractions. Here you can
promenade from one the-
matic area to the next:
they include an aviary, an
insectarium, a penguin
parade, a jungle scene and
performing dolphins. It lies
east of the M-40, well out
of the centre.
✉ Avenida de la
Democracia 50 ☎ 91
301 62 10 Ⓜ Valde-
bernardo 🚌 Nos 8 &
130 🕐 10am-9pm
⑤ adult/concession
€16.20/11.40 ♿ good

Parque de
Atracciones (2, M1)
This is a monster-sized
theme park with rides and
plenty of other diversions
for the kiddies, plus some
noisy, colourful shows during the summer months.
Those who have easily rat-
tled tummies should
beware.
✉ Casa de Campo
☎ 91 526 80 31

Babysitting & Childcare
Larger hotels (especially deluxe and top-end) will often have an in-house baby-
sitting service, and even medium-sized places have a reliable contact for such
things, starting at about €10 an hour and available at your hotel room. There is a
nursery (for children under six) at Barajas airport (T2) from 8am to 8pm. There are
also numerous advertisements for multilingual babysitters in the English-language
In Madrid publication.

Carousel Carousing

There's a carousel outside the El Corte Inglés department store at Calle Serrano 47. If you've dragged them to all the fine shops of Salamanca, don't they deserve a turn at something? €1.50 a pop. Big kids are allowed on too.

e www.parque deatracciones.es
M Batán ⏰ noon-10pm **$** €4.50

Parque Juan Carlos I (1, E4)

This is a large green space that's perfect for families with kids. It's located west of the Parque del Capricho, and has well-kept gardens dotted between fields. You'll see people flying kites, riding bikes, sailing remote-control boats on the water and just generally hanging out. From Tues-Fri in the evening, and on weekends and hols, there are train and catamaran rides (€3).
☎ 91 722 04 00
M Campo de las Naciones

Warner Brothers Movie World (1, E4)

About 25km south of central Madrid, this corporate entertainment festival (enter via Hollywood Boulevard) gives movie-savvy kids the chance to frolic with their celluloid pals.
✉ San Martín de la Vega **☎** 91 821 12 34
e www.warnerbros park.com **🚉** San Martín de la Vega
⏰ Wed-Sun 10am-midnight **$** adult/concession €32/24 for two consecutive days
♿ good

Zoo Aquarium Casa de Campo (2, M1)

Madrid's good zoo, housed in Casa de Campo, has over 3000 animals (there are even koalas!) and a decent aquarium with a better-than-average dolphin show. At night, there are guided tours of the aquarium and sound-and-light shows.
✉ Casa de Campo
☎ 91 512 37 80
e www.zoomadrid .com **M** Batán ⏰ Sun-Wed 10.30am-sunset, Thur-Sat 10.30am-midnight **$** adult/concession €12.15/9.80, free under-3
♿ good

Festival de Titeres

If you're in Madrid in July, and your kids are itching for a bit of culture, check out the great Festival of Puppet Theatre, with shows in the Parque del Buen Retiro (**M** Retiro) held throughout the month at 7.30pm & 10.30pm. Further information can be found at tourist offices (it's part of the Veranos de la Villa program) or by calling **☎** 610 38 51 98.

Something for the littlies at Parque de Buen Retiro p26

KEEPING FIT

Despite their love of food and drink, madrileños make looking good an art-form, and are prepared to exercise to keep themselves easy on the eye. The city itself, with its parks, pools, gyms and golf courses is a good place to keep your fitness regimen going. For more information, it's a good idea to contact the **Oficina de Información Deportiva** (☎ 91 540 39 39) or the **Consejo Superior Deportes** (☎ 91 589 67 00).

Cycling
'Madrid', as Fernando Martínez-Vidal (the city councillor in charge of traffic issues) once commented, 'is not a city for bicycles', but if you really need to get some pedal power, you can try the Parque Juan Carlos I (see p48), Casa de Campo (see p33) or the Parque del Buen Retiro (see p26).

Karacol Sports (2, O6; ✉ Calle de Tortosa 8, Huertas ☎ 91 539 96 33 e www.karacol.com) rents out mountain-bikes for €12 per day, and staff can help with information on spots outside of Madrid, where cycling is more of an attractive option. You'll need to bring photo ID with you to hire a bike.

Golf
Spaniards are golf-crazy, and it can be tricky to get a game on weekends and holidays. The peak season is October to March. Some clubs don't accept casual visitors.

Golf Park (1, D4; ✉ Parque Empresarial de la Moraleja ☎ 91 661 44 44 e www.golfpark.es, 9 holes from €17) is open to all comers and is in a business park north of the city along the N-I highway, beyond Paseo de la Castellana. Your own transport is the best way to get out here, otherwise grab a taxi.

Gym
Many of Madrid's deluxe and top-end hotels have work-out facilities for guests. Grab a list of *polideportivos* (sports centres) that have gyms from one of the tourist offices. The Chueca neighbourhood has a handful of gay-friendly gyms that accept casual visitors. Maps from the Berkana bookshop (see p61) have further details. The sports centres attached to the municipal swimming pools listed on the following page also offer casual aerobics classes and gym use.

Jogging
Madrid's parks have plenty of paths that can be used by joggers. Our favourite is the Campo del Moro (see p28), not just for its beauty, but also because it seems relatively undiscovered. Other parks that are popular with joggers include the Retiro (see p26), which has a designated jogging path; and the Casa de Campo (see p33), which is at its best early in the morning.

Swimming

Outdoor pools are open from June to September in several locations. During the rest of the year, indoor pools operate, as do some private pools that allow casual visits.

Piscinas Casa de Campo (2, M1; ✉ Avenida del Ángel, Casa de Campo ☎ 91 463 00 50, ⑤ adult/concession/over-65 €3.20/1.60/80c) has a great vibe, with all types jostling for space – families, preening narcissists, fitness fanatics and old folks taking a dip and a bit of sun (topless permitted).

Instalación Deportiva Municipal Chamartín (2, D8; ✉ Plaza de Perú ☎ 91 350 12 23, ⑤ adult/concession/over-65 €3.20/1.60/80c) has an indoor Olympic-sized (50m) swimming pool, although its location isn't particularly convenient for those staying centrally.

Hotel Emperador (3, D8; ✉ Gran Vía 53, Gran Vía ☎ 91 547 28 00, ⑤ Mon-Fri €19 Sat & Sun €29) is easily the city's swankiest place to swim, located on the rooftop and with marvellous views of the city. Non-guests are allowed to swim here.

Into the blue at Hotel Emperador

Tennis

Contact the organisations mentioned in this section's introduction (p49) for further details of public courts. Bringing your own equipment is a good idea.

Tennis Casa de Campo (2, M1; ✉ Casa de Campo ☎ 91 464 96 17, ⑤ adult/concession/over-65 €4.40/2/1) has extensive, quality tennis facilities. Courts can get heavily booked at weekends, so weekdays are a better idea.

Watersports

Madrid's landlocked status doesn't mean you can't partake in watersports – and thank heavens for that in summer!

Aquópolis (1, D3; ✉ Avenida de la Dehesa ☎ 91 815 69 11 e www.aquopolis.es, ⑤ adult/child €12.85/8.45), on the way to San Lorenzo de El Escorial (see p55), is a very large spot to indulge in water-slides, wave pools and other aquatic pursuits. Catch the bus from Moncloa. The park is in the suburb of Villanueva de la Cañada.

Boating Casa de Campo (2, M1; ✉ Casa de Campo ☎ 91 464 96 17, ⑤ €3.60 for up to 4 people for 45mins) is on the lake in this park. It has facilities for small boats, and is a relaxing way to get some peace and quiet. Ask at the information office near the lake for information about conditions and other details.

Flotarium (2, A8; ✉ Avenida Burgos 44, Chamartín ☎ 91 383 97 28 e www.flotarium.com, ⑤ €30 for 1hr 20mins) is a very relaxing form of sensory deprivation if Madrid's feast for the senses gets a little too over-whelming. It's probably not a great idea if you suffer from claustrophobia, however. Other relaxing treatments are also available.

out & about

WALKING TOURS
Los Austrias Stroll

From the grand 17th-century Plaza Mayor ❶, exit from the northwest corner and head left down Calle Mayor to historic Plaza de la Villa ❷, with Madrid's 17th-century *barroco madrileño (*Madrid baroque*) ayuntamiento* ❸ and Gothic-Mudéjar Casa de Los Lujanes ❹, one of the city's oldest surviving buildings. Follow cobbled Calle del Cordón to Calle de Segovia, where almost in front of you is the 15th-century Iglesia de San Pedro El Viejo ❺, with its Mudéjar tower. Walk down

Walk this way: the back of Plaza Mayor

distance 1.5km   duration 2½-3hrs
▶ start Ⓜ Sol (Plaza Mayor)
● end Ⓜ Sol (Plaza de San Miguel)

Costanilla de San Pedro to nicely restored Plaza de San Andrés ❻, which is the site of the Iglesia de San Andrés ❼. In nearby Plaza del Humiladero ❽, relax with a drink and snack, or take refreshments at any one of the tapas bars or traditional restaurants on Calle de la Cava Baja ❾, an atmospheric old street that follows the line of the city's former 12th-century wall, before venturing through Plaza Conde de Barajas. From the plaza, head up Calle de Miranda, finishing at the wrought-iron Mercado de San Miguel ❿ in Plaza de San Miguel.

Paseo del Prado

From Plaza de la Cibeles ❶, which separates Paseo del Prado from Paseo de los Recoletos and is encircled by the Palacio Buenavista ❷, the Banco de España, the Palacio de Linares ❸ – which once belonged to the prominent Alba family – and the Palacio de Comunicaciones ❹ – Madrid's impressive post office – head south on the left-hand side before turning left at Calle de Montalbán, where you'll find the Museo Nacional de Artes Decorativas ❺, former home of the Duchess of Santoña. Head back to Paseo del Prado, continuing south to Plaza de la Lealtad, where more grand architecture awaits, with the

Purpose-built Westin Palace

distance 1km **duration** 1½-2hrs
▶ **start** Ⓜ Banco de España (Plaza de la Cibeles)
● **end** 🚉 Atocha (Real Jardín Botánico)

city's *bolsa* (stock exchange) and the plush Hotel Ritz ❻, a heady example of early 20th-century style. A little further down, you come across the Plaza de Neptuno ❼ (so-named for its statue of the mythological sea king), which is bordered by the Museo Thyssen-Bornemisza ❽ as well as the mammoth Westin Palace ❾, which was built for the wedding of Alfonso XIII. From the plaza, you're within striking distance of the Museo del Prado ❿, with the Real Jardín Botánico ⓫ just across Plaza de Murillo, at the Prado's southern end.

Lavapiés

Not chock-full of tourist attractions, but filled with authentically grungy sights, sounds and smells, this is one of Madrid's most interesting neighbourhoods. Start at Plaza de Cascorro ➊ (once the scene of public executions) and walk south down Calle de Ebajadores. You'll pass El Rastro flea market, and soon come across the Iglesia de San Cayetano, a baroque church built over many years between the 17th and 18th centuries. Continuing down this street, turn left at Calle Sombrerete, then right at Calle de Mesón de Paredes, where you'll see the famous 19th-century tenement building of La Corrala ➋. Back on Calle Sombrerete, continue through to Plaza de Lavapiés – one of the best places to witness the festivities that take place in the neighbourhood for the Fiesta de la Virgen in August. From here, walk down Calle de Argumosa, a pleasant, tree-lined street with lots of nibbling options – we recommend the Casa de Tostas ➌. After this, turn left into Calle Dr Fourquet, then right at Calle de Santa Isabel.

SIGHTS & HIGHLIGHTS

La Corrala (pp43–4)
Casa de Tostas (p81)
Centro de Arte Reina Sofía (pp18–19)

Not a very hip flask – El Rastro market

Check out the barbershop tiles at No 22, then head south for the revamped hospital that now serves as the Centro de Arte Reina Sofía ➍.

---

distance 1.5km **duration** 1½hrs
▶ **start** Ⓜ La Latina (Plaza de Cascorro)
● **end** Ⓜ Atocha (Centro de Arte Reina Sofía)

Malasaña

Start this walk at the gates to the Palacio de Liria ❶, a glorious 1780 palace. From here, walk up Calle de Conde Duque, dominated by the enormous Centro Cultural Conde Duque ❷. Turn right at Plaza Guardia de Corps, into Calle Cristo, before turning left at Calle Bernardo López García, which will take you to Plaza de las Comendadores ❸ which has a cool Saturday afternoon market and the fine 17th-century Iglesia de las Comendadores de Santiago. From here, walk along Calle de Quiñones, turn left at Calle de San Bernardo and continue to Glorieta de Ruiz Jiménez, where you walk east to Glorieta de Bilbao. Pop into the Café Comercial ❹ to wet the whistle. That done, head down Calle de Manuela Malasaña, named after the local 19th-century seamstress who was a heroine of the city's brief 1808 anti-French uprising. Turn left at Calle de San Andrés, where you'll find some choice tilework, the best of which can be seen in the lively depictions of pharmaceutical cures at the corner of this street and Calle de San Vicente Ferrer. Hang a right at this last street and continue down Calle del Dos de Mayo to Plaza del Dos de Mayo ❺, the scene of fighting between angry *madrileños* and Joseph Bonaparte's troops on 2 May 1808.

SIGHTS & HIGHLIGHTS

Palacio de Liria (p44)
Centro Cultural Conde Duque (p96)
Plaza de las Comendadores (p69)
Café Comercial (p84)
Plaza del Dos de Mayo (p42)

Um, what are you doing son?

---

distance 1.75km **duration** 2hrs
▶ **start** Ⓜ Ventura Rodríguez (Palacio de Liria)
● **end** Ⓜ Tribunal (Plaza del Dos de Mayo)

EXCURSIONS
San Lorenzo de El Escorial   (1, D2)

Sheltering against the protective wall of the Sierra de Guadarrama and enjoying a healthy climate, the magnificent palace/monastery complex of San Lorenzo de El Escorial is a must-see. Felipe II had the complex built in the latter half of the 16th century, consisting of a huge monastery, royal palace and mausoleum (for his parents Carlos I and Isabel), all under the watchful eye of architect Juan de Herrera.

The main entrance lies on the west side. Above the gateway, a statue of San Lorenzo stands watch. Enter the Patio de los Reyes, which houses the statues of the six kings of Judah. Directly ahead lies the sombre basilica with its dark interior and wonderful statue of a crucified Christ, by Benvenuto Cellini.

Go back through the patio, turn right and follow the signs to the monastery and palace quarters. There are several rooms containing

> ### INFORMATION
> *50km northwest of Madrid*
> - 🚆 line C-8a from Atocha to El Escorial (€2.40 one way, 70mins, up to every 30mins), then 🚌 L1 (Circular) to San Lorenzo (95c, 5mins)
> - 🚌 661 (€2.70 one way, 1hr, every 20mins or so from Moncloa)
> - ☎ 91 890 59 02
> - e www.patrimonionacional.es
> - ① guided tour €6.90, audioguide €1.80; tourist office (☎ 91 890 53 13; Calle de Grimaldi 2; open Mon-Thur 10am-6pm, Fri-Sun 10am-7pm).
> - ② 1 Apr-30 Sept Tues-Sun 10am-9pm; 1 Oct-31 Mar Tues-Sun 10am-5pm
> - ⑤ adult/concession €6/3
> - ✗ in town

tapestries, one of which has El Greco's depiction of the martyrdom of San Mauricio. You'll soon reach the stupendous Hall of Battles, a long room with extraordinary depictions of military events running the length of the room and a beautiful barrel-vaulted ceiling painted in 1584. After this, go to the Palacio de los Austrias where you'll be able to imagine how Felipe II and his children lived. You then descend into the Panteón de los Reyes, where almost all of Spain's monarchs have been interred with their spouses. In the southeastern corner of the complex, the chapterhouses contain a minor treasure-trove of works by El Greco, Titian, Tintoretto and Bosch.

The orderly gardens just south of the monastery can also be visited.

The green, green gardens of San Lorenzo de El Escorial

Toledo (1, G2)

Once set to become the capital of a united Spain, Toledo is a remarkably beautiful city, and *the* place to come for architectural history. With evidence of the Jewish, Muslim and Christian presence (all of whom lived in relative harmony), and such a concentration of Spain's artistic legacy, Toledo really does knock your socks off.

The city is built on a hill around which the Río Tajo flows on three sides. Modern suburbs spread beyond the river and walls of the old town *(casco antiguo)*. However when you arrive, sooner or later, you'll end up at Plaza de Zocodover, the main square of the old town, from where a medieval labyrinth of streets spreads out in a confusing manner.

Just south of the plaza is the alcazar – originally a Muslim fortress in the 10th century, and later rebuilt as a royal residence for Carlos I. Just outside what were once the Arab walls, you'll find the **Museo de Santa Cruz** (☎ 925 22 10 36, Calle de Cervantes 3, open 10am-2pm, €2) a 16th-century former hospital that holds several El Greco paintings. And if that whets your appetite, you should head to Toledo's stunning **cathedral** (☎ 925 22 22 41; Calle de Cardenal Cisneros; open 10.30am-6.30pm, €4.80) an essentially Gothic structure that (in the 13th century) replaced the central mosque. Inside you'll find the Capilla de la Torre and the sacristy, where another collection of El Greco's works exists. El Greco's masterpiece *The Burial of the Count of Orgaz* can be seen in Iglesia de Santo Tomé. And if that's still not enough, go to the **Casa y Museo de El Greco** (☎ 925 22 40 46; Calle de Samuel Levi; open Tues-Sat 10am-2pm & 4-6pm, Sun 10am-2pm; €1.20).

INFORMATION

70km south of Madrid

- 🚆 Chamartín or Atocha stations (€4.80 one way, 8 to 10 daily)
- 🚌 Galiano Continental buses from Estación Sur (€3.65 one way, 50mins, every hour or so from 6.30am-10pm)
- ⓘ tourist office (☎ 925 22 08 43; fax 925 25 26 48; open Mon-Sat 9am-7pm & Sun 9am-3pm), just outside the Puerta Nueva de Bisagra; information office (open Mon 10.30am-2.30pm, Tues-Sun 10.30am-2.30pm & 4.30-7pm) in the *Ayuntamiento* (town hall)
- ✕ in town

Toledo town

Real Palacio de Aranjuez (1, F4)

Aranjuez is something of a haven from the capital. Once a royal playground, the palace and its meticulously maintained gardens are accessible to the public and make a popular weekend getaway. The town of Aranjuez is pleasant too, and has a reputation for producing juicy strawberries, which are sold throughout town.

The palace started life as a relatively modest summer residence for Felipe II, and was converted into an architectural extravaganza by the 18th century. With Versailles (the palatial benchmark for much of Europe) in mind, the palace has over 300 rooms and lots of glitz. Rooms of note include one covered in mirrors and a stunning octagonal smoking room kitted out 'Alhambra-style'. Don't forget to wander around the gardens either – a nice natural antidote to decor overload.

INFORMATION

48km south of Madrid
- 🚉 line C3 from Atocha to Aranjuez (€2.60 one way, 45mins, at least hourly), then a signposted 10min walk
- 🚌 Autominibus Urbanos (☎ 91 527 12 94, €2.60 one way, 1hr, every 30mins or so)
- ☎ 91 891 07 40
- 🄴 www.patrimonionacional.es
- ⓘ tourist office (☎ 91 891 04 27; 🄴 www.aranjuez.net; Plaza de San Antonio 9; open 1 Oct-31 Mar Tues-Sat 10am-1pm & 3-5pm, Sun 10am-2pm; 1 Apr-30 Sept Tues-Sat 10am-2pm & 4-6pm, Sun 10am-2pm)
- 🕐 1 Oct-31 Mar Tues-Sun 10am-5.15pm, 1 Apr-30 Sept 10am 6.15pm
- 💲 adult/concession €4.80/2.40, free under-5 & Wed for EU citizens
- ✗ in town

Real Palacio de El Pardo (1, D3)

This is the nearest regal retreat to Madrid, with a large palace that seems almost deserted much of the time. The site was attractive to Madrid's monarchs due to its excellent hunting (you'll see plenty of animal-related traffic signs on the trip out here), and made even more attractive by the royal palace constructed for King Felipe II. The current palace was designed by Francesco Sabatini after the original was destroyed by fire in the 18th century. It was used as a residence by General Franco until his death, and there are compulsory tours (Spanish-language) of the interior. State rooms are the usual mix of gilt, tapestry, silk and chandeliers, but Franco's brown-hued bathroom would have to be one of the more interesting stops.

INFORMATION

15km northwest of Madrid
- 🚌 601 (€1, 25mins, every 15 mins from Moncloa)
- ✉ Carretera de El Pardo
- ☎ 91 376 15 00
- 🄴 www.patrimonionacional.es
- 🕐 Mon-Sat 10.30am-6.45pm, Sun & hols 9.30am-2.30pm
- 💲 adult/concession €3/1.50, free under-5 & Wed for EU citizens
- ✗ in town

ORGANISED TOURS

The **Patronato Municipal de Turismo** organises myriad walks around Madrid. You can get information about them from any Caja de Madrid bank and its office at Plaza Mayor 3 (3, H8; ☎ 91 588 16 36; ⓔ infor turismo@munimadrid.es;), as well as information about other organised tours throughout the city. Keep your eyes peeled for privately run tours and the services of guides in the local press.

Bravo Bike (3, F10)
Fancy a bike tour of Madrid, or further afield? Bravo Bike can help you out. The one-day tour is a nice blend of the urban and the outdoors.
✉ **Calle de la Montera 25** ☎ **91 640 12 98**
⑤ from €55

Madrid Vision
Backed by the *ayuntamiento*, these red double-decker buses show visitors the sights. There are three routes, frequent stops and you can buy tickets on board.
☎ **91 779 18 88**
⊙ late-Jun–late-Sep 9.30am-midnight
⑤ adult/concession €9.60/4.80 (€1.20 surcharge weekends & hols)

Paseo por el Madrid del Capitán Alatriste
(3, H8) Fans of sword-wielding 17th-century

literary hero Capitán Alatriste will enjoy discovering his haunts. The tour is conducted in English and Spanish. Buy tickets 30mins before.
✉ **Plaza Mayor 3**
☎ **91 588 16 36** ⊙ Fri 9.30pm ⑤ €3

Paseo por el Madrid de los Austrias
(3, H8) This handy tour (in Spanish and English) is organised by the *patronato*, and is a great introduction to Habsburg Madrid's sights. Buy tickets 30mins before the tour departs.
✉ **Plaza Mayor 3**
☎ **91 588 16 36**
⊙ Sat 10am ⑤ €3

Paseo por el Parque del Retiro (2, M6)
This is a good group stroll through Madrid's green lung. There's commentary in English and Spanish, and it's all under the aegis of the *patronato*. Buy tickets

30mins before from Caja de Madrid or information offices.
✉ **Puerta del Alcalá entrance** ☎ **91 588 16 36** ⊙ Fri 10am ⑤ €3

Pullmantur (3, F6)
Mainstream tours are offered, with daytime jaunts, night tours, dinner-and-show trips, as well as excursions further afield; they can also organise a bullfight visit for you.
✉ **Plaza de Oriente 8**
☎ **91 541 18 07**
⑤ from €12

Tapas Walking Tour
(3, J14) One interesting guided tour is this tapas crawl, run by Olé Spain. Various other tours (group and individual) are offered that go to a range of other cities.
✉ **Paseo Infanta Isabel 21** ☎ **91 551 52 94**

Don't forget to duck – Madrid Vision bus

shopping

Madrid's shopping, whether you intended to indulge or not, will compete with many of the city's famous sites for your attention. From small local-craft shops and slick modernist fashion temples to old-fashioned food stores and full-to-bursting department stores and malls, Madrid will impress you with the quality of goods on offer, the generally reasonable prices and the courteous service that never descends to obsequiousness. Prepare to stretch your credit card and those airline baggage restrictions to the limit!

Chueca is an excellent shopping precinct, with Calle del Almirante, Calle de Fuencarral and Calle Piamonte full of fashionable shops. **Salamanca** is like Chueca's grown-up sister, with more expensive, conservative (yet still chic!) tastes catered for, especially on Calle de Serrano.

For gifts and items typical of Madrid, the shops around Plaza Mayor and Plaza de Puerta del Sol have some colourful window displays and a wealth of goodies. And of course, there's always the famous El Rastro.

Opening Times

Most shops are open Monday to Saturday 10am to 2pm and 5 to 8pm, although many businesses only open for the morning on Saturday. Traditional shops almost always observe the siesta, while modern ones and those on main shopping streets stay open all day. Almost all shops are closed on Sunday, unless they sell items of 'cultural significance', such as books. Some stores in the city centre operate on a rotating system of Sundays, with times signposted in the window.

ANTIQUES & CRAFTS

Agustin (3, K8)
A delightful trip back in time, Agustin is a tiny shop that sells antique *trajes de luce* (bullfighter suits), bullfighting posters, gloriously colourful capes and shawls, and quaint postcards. It's handy to the Rastro markets too, and noticeably more peaceful.
✉ **Calle de Rodas 28, La Latina** ☎ **91 467 87 50** Ⓜ **La Latina**
🕐 **Mon-Fri noon-2.30pm & 6-8.30pm, Sat & Sun noon-2.30pm**

Antigua Casa Talavera (3, E7)
Talavera is a Castilian town famous for its ceramics, and there are plenty of examples of the town's talent here, as well as from other parts of Spain. It's absolutely full to bursting with breakables, so don't act like a bull in a china shop.
✉ **Calle de Isabel la Católica 2, Sol & Gran Vía** ☎ **91 547 34 17**

Ⓜ **Santo Domingo** 🕐 **Mon-Fri 10am-1.30pm & 5-8pm, Sat 10am-1.30pm**

Galerías Piquer
(3, K8) If you'd like to do the bulk of your antique shopping under one roof, this centre is a good start. There are about 70 antique shops here, of varying quality and scope, but handy to El Rastro on Sunday. Hours may differ from shop to shop, with some closing for August.
✉ **cnr Calle Ribera de Curtidores & Calle de Rodas, La Latina** Ⓜ **Puerta de Toledo** 🕐 **Mon-Fri 10.30am-2pm & 5-8pm, Sat & Sun 10.30am-2pm**

La Pepa (3, D13)
A lavender-tinted jewellery box of a store, La Pepa is charming for its cuteness and its stock, which consists of old-fashioned trinkets in very good knick: hats, ashtrays, baubles and

VAT Refund
Value-added tax (VAT) is known as IVA in Spain. On accommodation and restaurant prices, it's 7% (usually included in prices). On retail goods it's 16%, and you're entitled to a refund of the 16% IVA on purchases from the one retailer totalling more than €90, if you take the goods out of the EU within three months. Ask for a Cashback form when you make a purchase, show your passport and then present the form at the customs booth for IVA refunds when you depart Spain. You'll need your passport and proof that you're leaving the EU.

all sorts of gifts with a difference. Service comes with a smile and a *violeta* (lolly).
✉ **Calle de Gravina 12, Chueca** ☎ **92 532 18 48** Ⓜ **Chueca** 🕐 **Mon-Sat 11am-2pm & 5-9pm**

Lladró (4, J9)
That much sought-after and coveted Lladró figurine your mum's been aching for can be found here. A veritable menagerie of lonely shepherds, imploring children and beatific virgins awaits placement in the *objets d'art* cabinet.
✉ **Calle de Serrano 68, Salamanca** ☎ **91 435 51 12** Ⓜ **Serrano or Nuñez de Balboa** 🕐 **Mon-Sat 10am-8pm**

Got to get past the rhino at Galerías Piquer

BOOKS

Berkana (3, C11)
With a strong selection of gay literature, gifts and videos, Berkana is a must-visit, with lots of good information about Madrid's gay scene available, plus a café.
✉ **Calle de Hortaleza 61, Chueca ☎ 91 522 55 99 ⓜ Chueca** ⏰ **Mon-Fri 10.30am-9pm, Sat 11.30am-9pm & Sun noon-2pm & 5-9pm**

FNAC (3, E9)
This large, French-owned store not only stocks a very solid range of Spanish-language books of all descriptions, but also has French- and English-language publications, CDs and concert/event tickets.
✉ **Calle de Preciados 28, Sol ☎ 91 520 00 00 ⓜ Callao** ⏰ **Mon-Sat 10am-9.30pm, Sun & hols noon-9.30pm**

The International Bookshop (3, E7)
If you're after second-hand books that you won't mind disposing of or that you might like to add to your collection, The International Bookshop has loads, predominantly in English.
✉ **Calle de Campomanes 13, Sol & Gran Vía ☎ 91 541 72 91 ⓜ Santo Domingo or Ópera** ⏰ **Mon-Fri 11am-2.30pm & 4.30-8.30pm, Sat 11am-2.30pm & 4.30-7.30pm**

La Casa del Libro (3, E10) Madrid's leading bookshop stocks a wide selection of books on all manner of subjects, with some in French, some in English, and plenty in Spanish.
✉ **Gran Vía 29–31, Gran Vía ☎ 91 521 22 19 ⓜ Gran Vía** ⏰ **Mon-Sat 9.30am-9.30pm**

Librería Booksellers (4, F7) You'll find plenty of English-language titles here, which is probably the best place for books if English is your mother tongue. Helpful staff will ease any decision-making dilemmas.
✉ **Calle de José Abascal 48, Chamberí ☎ 91 442 79 59 ⓜ Alonso Cano** ⏰ **Mon-Fri 9.30am-2pm & 5-8pm, Sat 10am-2pm**

Librería de Mujeres (3, G9) There's a good range of literature by women, books dealing with feminism, and plenty of non-fiction titles about women's issues here.
✉ **Calle de San Cristóbal 17, Los**

FYI: FNAC

Local Books
The immensely popular Arturo Perez-Reverte has written a few books set in Madrid, which make great accompaniments to a visit. Try *The Flanders Panel*, an art-world thriller; *The Fencing Master*, a historical mystery; or the trilogy based on the adventures of the sword-fighting 17th-century Capitán Alatriste.

Austrias ☎ 91 523 23 20 ⓜ Sol ⏰ **Mon-Fri 10am-2pm & 5-8pm, Sat 10am-2pm**

Panta Rhei (3, B12)
This friendly bookshop has a plethora of tomes specialising in art, design, illustration and photography – and they look good enough to eat. You can also view well-selected drawings in the gallery.
✉ **Calle de Pelayo 68, Chueca ☎ 91 319 89 02 ⓜ Chueca** ⏰ **Mon-Fri 10.30am-2.30pm & 5-9pm, Sat 10.30am-2.30pm & 5-8pm**

Second-hand Bookstalls (3, K15)
Just near the Real Jardín Botánico, this is not a bad little strip to bag some interesting reading. It can be a bit of a trash-or-treasure hunt.
✉ **Cuesta de Claudio Moyano, Jerónimos ⓜ Atocha** ⏰ **10am-2pm & 5-8pm**

DEPARTMENT & CONVENIENCE STORES

ABC Serrano (4, H9)
Housed in a beautiful Mudéjar-style building in fashionable Salamanca, this excellent mall has five levels of shops (men's and women's fashion, homewares, gifts) and a space for eating.
✉ **Calle de Serrano 61, Salamanca ☎ 91 577 50 31 Ⓜ Rubén Dario** ⏰ **Mon-Sat 10am-8.30pm**

ABC Serrano

El Corte Inglés (3, F9)
Behold the mother lode! A national institution and the embodiment of the one-stop shop, El Corte Inglés deserves a round of applause for seeming to stock everything you could possibly think of. Clothes, underwear, footwear,

El Jardín de Serrano

books, music, tickets for various events, electrical appliances and furnishings are all represented, and there are well over a dozen branches throughout town.
✉ **Calle Preciados 1, Sol ☎ 91 418 88 00 Ⓜ Sol** ⏰ **Mon-Sat 10am-10pm**

El Jardín de Serrano (2, L6) As shopping malls go, this one's in the small but perfectly formed category. It's high-end stuff, and mostly covering the fashion side, with a smattering of accessories. Pop into the Mallorca café to refuel on tea and cakes, all while gazing at the garden.
✉ **Calle Goya 6, Salamanca ☎ 91 577 00 12 Ⓜ Serrano** ⏰ **Mon-Sat 10am-10pm**

Marks & Spencer (4, K9) Marks & Spencer is a popular spot for homesick English expats and *madrileños*. You'll find the usual M&S goodies, plus foodstuffs. It's not quite in the same league as El Corte Inglés, though.
✉ **Calle de Serrano 52, Salamanca ☎ 91 520 00 00 Ⓜ Serrano** ⏰ **daily 10am-8.30pm**

Moda Shopping (4, A8) There are plenty of boutiques here to get you outfitted for whatever Madrid's weather dishes out. There's also a strong showing from some of the nicer homeware chains.
✉ **Avenida del General Perón 40, Complejo Azca Ⓜ Santiago Bernabéu** ⏰ **Mon-Sat 10am-9.30pm**

VIPS (3, D8)
You might shudder at the idea of coming to a shopping mecca like Madrid and having to visit a convenience store, but hey, we've all got to do it at some point. VIPS branches are scattered throughout the city, with a range of items. This is where you'll find those damn toenail clippers you forgot to pack.
✉ **Gran Vía 43, Gran Vía ☎ 91 559 66 21 Ⓜ Callao or Santo Domingo** ⏰ **Mon-Fri 8am-2am; Sat, Sun & hols 9am-2am**

DESIGN, HOMEWARES & GIFTS

Alambique (3, E6)
The sort of people who can't get enough gadgets and utensils in their kitchen will love this place. You can find glassware, pots, pans and cutlery. Cooking classes can also be arranged – great if you speak Spanish.
✉ **Plaza de la Encarnación 2, Sol & Gran Vía** ☎ **91 547 42 20** Ⓜ **Santo Domingo or Ópera** ⏲ **Mon-Sat 10am-2pm & 5-8pm**

A teaser of what's in store - Objetos de Arte Toledano

Listas de Boda
Listas de boda (wedding registries) are wedding-happy Madrid's answer to nuptial gift-giving dilemmas. Many of the city's stores display a sign advertising the service, and these shops can be excellent places to look for homeware-related presents for yourself (and anyone else).

Batavia (3, A12)
Batavia brings a world of stylish furniture and homewares to Madrid, particularly from Asia. Countries of origin include China, Indonesia, India and Vietnam. There are also paintings, silk fabrics and porcelain objects in both antique and modern designs.
✉ **Calle de Serrano Anguita 4, Chueca** ☎ **91 448 75 63** Ⓜ **Alonso Martínez** ⏲ **Mon-Fri 10am-2.30pm & 5-8.30pm, Sat 10.30am-2pm & 5-8pm**

Casa Yustas (3, G8)
Gift shopping can be a real pain. Buy something practical or buy something emblematic of where you've been? You can actually cover both bases with *castizo* (true-blue madrileño) caps in all sizes and ceramic homewares. You can also find some laughably kitsch stuff if you want to provoke hilarity back home.
✉ **Plaza Mayor 30, Los Austrias** ☎ **91 366 50 84** Ⓜ **Sol** ⏲ **Mon-Sat 9.30am-9.30pm, Sun & hols 11am-9.30pm**

Fann (2, L7)
Fann is a bright and colourful shop that specialises in prints and posters and a range of beautifully coloured stationery.
✉ **Calle de Velázquez 24, Retiro** ☎ **91 435 72 23** Ⓜ **Velázquez** ⏲ **Mon-Sat 10am-2pm & 5-8pm**

Musgo (2, L6)
Something of a riot of colour and texture, Musgo shops stock bohemian-inspired homewares and gifts, with plenty of soft furnishings in natural fibres. There are also shoes, bags and clothes for sale.
✉ **Calle de Serrano 18, Salamanca** ☎ **91 575 33 50** Ⓜ **Serrano** ⏲ **Mon-Sat 10.15am-8.30pm**

Objetos de Arte Toledano (3, H13)
An enormous emporium of Spanish arts, crafts and kitsch awaits shoppers just near the Prado. Yep, it's touristy, but it's also fun and the range is huge.
✉ **Paseo del Prado 10, Huertas** ☎ **91 429 50 00** Ⓜ **Banco de España** ⏲ **Mon-Sat 9.30am-8pm**

Stone Designs (3, H6)
This perky, airy studio contains some of Madrid's spaciest and out-there homewares and gifts. Colours are bold, designs are beautiful, yet everything has a purpose, and prices are more than reasonable.
✉ **Calle del Cordón 10, Los Austrias** ☎ **91 540 03 36** Ⓜ **Ópera** ⏲ **Mon-Sat 10am-2pm & 4-8pm**

FASHION, CLOTHES & SHOES

Adolfo Dominguez
(2, L6) When we popped in, Adolfo Dominguez was doing a brisk trade with those wanting well-made, stylish clothes in natural fibres, with the odd twist thrown in. The shop itself is akin to an airy temple of minimalism.
✉ Calle de Serrano 18, Salamanca ☎ 91 577 82 80 Ⓜ Serrano ⊙ Mon-Sat 10am-8.30pm

Camper (3, D8)
Fight the hordes of Spaniards seeking comfort, and American college students seeking cool, to get to these shoes. With innovative designs, sturdy construction and all the colours of the rainbow represented, a visit here ensures you're a happy Camper. There's also a branch at Calle de Preciados 23.
✉ Gran Vía 54, Gran Vía ☎ 91 547 52 23 Ⓜ Sol ⊙ Mon-Sat 10am-2pm & 5-8.30pm

Cortefiel (2, L7)
Cortefiel is good for clothes more suited to business than pleasure. Clothes maintain a fashionable edge to stop them looking too conservative, and a good range of accessories and leather goods can help with outfit-update crises.
✉ Calle Goya 29, Retiro ☎ 91 577 55 05 Ⓜ Velázquez ⊙ Mon-Sat 10am-8.30pm

Dresscode (3, D12)
Not for shy and retiring types, the *haute* end of men's fashion gets a serious work-out here (as do credit cards), with beautifully cut garments for those who like to be noticed.
✉ Calle de Augusto Figueroa 16, Chueca ☎ 91 531 64 79 Ⓜ Chueca ⊙ Tues-Sat 11am-2pm & 5-9pm, Mon 6-9pm

Ekseption (2, K7)
Spain's most exclusive boutique has all the big names that 'fashionistas' love: Marni, Prada, Chloe, Dries Van Noten, Jean-Paul Gaultier and Dolce & Gabbana. You enter via a sleek Zen-style pebbled walkway and you depart with a serious case of fashionitis.
✉ Calle Velázquez 28, Retiro ☎ 91 577 45 53 Ⓜ Velázquez ⊙ Mon-Sat 10.30am-2.30pm & 5-9pm

Excrupulous Net
(3, D13) The shoes here tend towards the very well-made and the imaginative, with a great range from the excellent Muxart (Barcelona) brand. There are shoes for men and women, plus a range of bags too.
✉ Calle Almirante 7, Chueca ☎ 91 521 72 44 Ⓜ Chueca ⊙ Mon-Sat 11am-2pm & 5.30-8.30pm

Farrutx (2, L6)
The antithesis of Camper shoes, Farrutx is where you come for flashy, killer heels that make you wonder if you'll be able to walk more than five metres once they're on. There's a range of bags on offer as well, and a few party-pooping flats.
✉ Calle de Serrano 7, Salamanca ☎ 91 577

Need a H.A.N.D? p65

09 24 Ⓜ Retiro
🕐 Mon-Sat 10am-2pm
& 5.30-8.30pm

H.A.N.D (3, D11)
Short for Have A Nice Day
(shudder), but not at all
cheesy. The clothes here
lean towards the smarter
end of whatever's in fashion in France at this very
minute. It's a nice-looking
shop too, with some interesting colours and textures
scattered about.
✉ **Calle de Hortaleza
26, Chueca** ☎ 91 521
51 52 Ⓜ **Gran Vía**
🕐 Mon-Sat 11am-9pm

Lanikai (4, K3)
A three-storey palace of
street-, skatewear and
snowboarding gear.
Trainers (often limited edi-
tion) are bountiful, and you
can also buy records and
CDs here.
✉ **Calle Alberto
Aguilera 1, Malasaña**
☎ 91 591 34 13
Ⓜ **San Bernardo**
🕐 Mon-Sat 10.30am-
9pm

Lo Stivale (3, C13)
Men who want good qual-
ity shoes should head
straight here, where some
very stylish Italian numbers
jostle for your attention. The
store itself is very attractive
too, which makes it easier
for anyone in your company
who's hanging around waiting for a decision.
✉ **Calle de Piamonte
14, Chueca** ☎ 91 531
18 01 Ⓜ **Chueca**
🕐 Mon-Sat 11am-2pm
& 5-9pm

Matane (3, B13)
Matane is a groovy little
shop with some interesting
design touches, but of
greater interest is the

Clubbing Clobber
Calle de Fuencarral is easily *the* place to get kitted out
for Madrid's clubs. There are dozens of shops, many
featuring very little in the way of natural fibres or
sombre colours. The shops themselves are easy to find
– they sound just like the nightclubs and are just as
loud. Check the quality of some of the garments, as
they can get quite pawed. The best place to look is
Mercado Fuencarral, which stocks better-quality stuff.

selection of Europe's riskier
designers. The accessories
are excellent too.
✉ **Calle de
Campoamor 9, Chueca**
☎ 91 319 19 90
Ⓜ **Alonso Martínez**
🕐 Mon-Fri 10.30am-
2pm & 5-8.30pm, Sat
11am-2pm & 5-8.30pm

Mercado Fuencarral
(3, C11) A one-stop collection of shops for those
itching to get their hands
on streetwear and rave-
friendly fashions. Shoes,
tops, bottoms, jewellery,
sunglasses, bags and music
can all be found, and a

range of budgets can be
catered to. Plus, it beats
some of the tackier outlets
on this particular strip.
✉ **Calle de Fuencarral
45, Chueca** ☎ 91 521
41 52 Ⓜ **Tribunal**
🕐 Mon-Sat 11am-9pm

Mitsouko (3, C11)
Billing itself as a
'fashion/press/music/design/
cafe' sort of place,
Mitsouko has some slick
designer clothes for club-
bing or chilling out, coffee-
table books on fashion and
photography, and a little
bar with an espresso
machine and bottles of

Made for walkin' – Mercado Fuencarral

Busy, busy Zara

alcohol; it has other branches too.

✉ **Calle de Fuencarral 59, Chueca** ☎ **91 701 08 35** Ⓜ **Tribunal** ⏲ **Mon-Sat 10.30am-9pm**

Pedro del Hierro

(2, L6) The typical Pedro del Hierro look revolves around elegant, low-key designs (for men and women) with high-quality fabrics and finishes. This shop is also a good spot for ties, shoes and bags.

✉ **Calle de Serrano 24, Salamanca** ☎ **91 575 69 06** Ⓜ **Serrano** ⏲ **Mon-Sat 10am-8.30pm**

Purificación García

(2, L6) The business-like clothes (albeit featuring interesting fabrics and colours) are allowed to shine in this modern lay-out. It's a good place for quality, special-occasion outfits.

✉ **Calle de Serrano 28, Salamanca** ☎ **91 435 80 13** Ⓜ **Serrano** ⏲ **Mon-Sat 10am-8.30pm**

Sportivo (3, A7)

Label-lovin' casuals will want to move in here. Labels include Duffer of St George, Oeuf, Burro and Pringle. The range of shirts is particularly appealing, as is the decor.

✉ **Calle de Conde Duque 20, Malasaña** ☎ **91 542 56 61** Ⓜ **Noviciados** ⏲ **Mon-Sat 10am-2pm & 4-9pm**

The Deli Room

(3, C10) With goods displayed like, you guessed it, a deli, we were hooked from the first moment. The stock consists of cutting-edge Spanish designers out to make a statement. Look out for the Ailanto label in particular.

✉ **Calle de Santa Bárbara 4, Malasaña** ☎ **91 521 1983** Ⓜ **Tribunal** ⏲ **Mon-Fri 10.30am-2pm & 5-9pm, Sat 11am-2pm & 5-8.30pm**

Underground (2, O3)

With that authentic vintage-clothing store smell, Underground is a groovy place to scour the racks for preloved ball-gowns, suede jackets, old-fashioned heels and funky tops. You'll find fashions

from the 1950s to the very recent for men and women alike, plus some new stuff.

✉ **Calle Mira el Río Baja 14, Rastro** ☎ **91 364 15 46** Ⓜ **Puerta de Toledo** ⏲ **Mon-Fri 10am-2.30pm & 5.30-8.30pm, Sat 10am-2.30pm, Sun & hols 10.30am-3.30pm**

Zara (3, E10)

This chain has branches all over Madrid. Zara's recipe for success involves churning out fashion-conscious knock-offs of designer collections for men, women and children at very affordable prices, without the stain of sweatshop labour. The store's popularity means that items can get severely mauled, so before you buy check things such as buttons, collars, zips and seams.

✉ **Gran Vía 32, Gran Vía** ☎ **91 522 97 27** Ⓜ **Gran Vía** ⏲ **10am-8.30pm**

Rebajas!

Anyone with an eye for a bargain will be salivating if they visit Madrid during sale time. Look for the word *rebajas* and get ready to exercise those credit cards. Everything is marked down from around mid-January to the end of February, and from the beginning of July until the end of August, with the discounts increasing as the sales draw to their conclusion (although the really good stuff gets snapped up very quickly!).

FOOD & DRINK

Bombonería Santa
(4, K9) A sweet tooth should be indulged at regular intervals, and this lovely shop will give you (and your dentist) plenty to work with. Selections can be packaged in gift boxes, which are almost as edible-looking as their contents.
✉ **Calle de Serrano 56, Salamanca** ☎ **91 576 86 46** Ⓜ **Nuñez de Balboa** ⏰ **Mon-Sat 10am-2pm & 5-8.30pm**

Casa Mira (3, G11)
Turrón, a nutty nougat treat that's queued for at Christmas-time, can be tracked down here. Locals say it's the best, and we're inclined to agree, as the business has been in the same family's hands since 1842.
✉ **Carrera de San Jerónimo 30, Huertas** ☎ **91 429 88 95** Ⓜ **Sevilla** ⏰ **10am-2pm & 5-9pm**

La Bio Tika (3, J12)
Attached to the restaurant of the same name, La Bio Tika stocks macrobiotic grains, nuts and cereals. There are also soy products, plus a range of gluten-free edibles.
✉ **Calle Amor de Dios 3, Huertas** ☎ **91 429 07 80** Ⓜ **Antón Martín** ⏰ **Mon-Fri 10am-11.30pm; Sat, Sun & hols 1-5pm & 7-11.30pm**

Lavinia (4, J10)
This capacious, well-equipped store will set you right in your search for the perfect Spanish drop. You can also find wines from around the world. If you've

mmmm Mallorca

remembered to pack your own bottle opener, you might like to wander to the park for an alfresco tipple.
✉ **Calle de José Ortega y Gasset 16, Salamanca** ☎ **91 426 06 04** ⏰ **Mon-Sat 10am-9pm**

Mallorca (4, K10)
A fantastic spot to pick up delicious goodies as gifts or as snacks on the run, Mallorca has a great range of cheeses, meats, pastries, alcohol and some mouth-watering tapas. You pay for your goods at the cash register, handing over a small plastic board where purchases have been recorded. Ingenious!
✉ **Calle de Velázquez 59, Salamanca** ☎ **91 431 99 09** Ⓜ **Núñez de Balboa** ⏰ **9.30am-9pm**

Museo del Jamón
(3, G10) Only the Spanish can call a ham shop a 'museo', but then again, it looks like every single pig

in Spain has donated a leg. There are branches throughout the city, and it's a good place to assuage hunger pains (vegetarians look elsewhere!) or ponder how to get a big fat pig leg through customs.
✉ **Carrera de San Jerónimo 6, Huertas** ☎ **91 521 03 46** Ⓜ **Sol** ⏰ **Mon-Sat 9am-midnight, Sun 10am-midnight**

Patrimonio Cultural Olivarero (3, B12)
Pedro Rodrigo knows his oil, and so will you if you spend enough time here. Bottles of golden and green olive oil from all over Spain are all you'll find here. It almost makes you wish you'd smuggled in some bread.
✉ **Calle Mejia Lequerica 1, Chueca** ☎ **91 308 05 05** Ⓜ **Alonso Martínez** ⏰ **Mon-Fri 10am-2pm & 5-8pm, Sat 10am-2pm**

FOR CHILDREN

Caramelos Paco
(3, J8) Much as you tell them 'it'll rot your teeth', kids will be drawn to this treasure-trove of sweets, sweets and more sweets. And they are indeed delicious, although anyone who dreads putting kids to bed in the midst of a sugar rush might want to time their visit here accordingly.
✉ **Calle de Toledo 53, Los Austrias** ☎ **91 365 42 58** Ⓜ **La Latina**
⏲ **Mon-Sat 9.30am-2pm & 5-8.30pm**

Dideco (2, O3)
Stock up on kids' toys (many of which may appeal to grown-ups) at Dideco, where you'll find everything from mini-roller skates, inflatable pools, educational games, bath toys and art supplies. There are two other branches in Madrid.
✉ **Mercado Puerta de Toledo, Ronda de Toledo 1, Rastro** ☎ **91 365 02 40** Ⓜ **Puerta de Toledo** ⏲ **Tues-Sat 10.30am-9pm, Sun 10.30am-2.30pm**

El Tintero Niños
(3, C12) Hunt out imaginative and colourful slogan T-shirts and romper suits for the baby or wee nipper in your life. Our favourite? A red romper suit emblazoned with the phrase 'Enfant Terrible'. Grown-ups can shop at No 5.
✉ **Calle Gravina 9, Chueca** ☎ **91 310 44 02** Ⓜ **Chueca** ⏲ **10.30am-2pm & 5-9pm**

Fiestas Paco (3, K7)
Jam-packed with all the prerequisites for a rip-snorter of a party, this is *the* place to come for lurid wigs, games and other sundries that will keep the littlies distracted for 10 minutes or so.
✉ **Calle de Toledo 52, Los Austrias** ☎ **91 365 27 60** Ⓜ **La Latina**

⏲ **Mon-Fri 9.30am-2pm & 5-8.30pm, Sat 9.30am-2pm**

Marquitos (4, J9)
Kids' feet grow so fast, and if a Bigfoot-in-the-making is on holiday with you, you can snap up snazzy little shoes at this shop.
✉ **Calle de Serrano 70, Salamanca** ☎ **91 576 33 84** Ⓜ **Nuñez de Balboa or Serrano** ⏲ **Mon-Sat 10am-2pm & 5-8.30pm**

Prénatal (4, J3)
Madrid loves kids, and there are several branches of this popular chain throughout the city (including Calle de Goya 99). It's a good place to find colourful kids' wear, plus mothering essentials and mother-to-be products.
✉ **Calle de San Bernardo 97, Chamberí** ☎ **91 594 24 00** Ⓜ **San Bernardo** ⏲ **10am-8pm**

JEWELLERY, PERFUME & ACCESSORIES

Carrera y Carrera
(2, K6) Providing chunky diamonds and other precious-stone jawbreaker rings and jewels to the good ladies of Madrid since 1885, this store is known for service that is so silky smooth that staff will always be courteous and charming even if you're obviously in the 'just looking' demographic.
✉ **Calle de Serrano 27, Salamanca** ☎ **91 577 05 72** Ⓜ **Serrano** ⏲ **Mon-Sat 10am-2pm & 4.30-8.30pm**

Mott (3, C13)
Run by stylish and sweetly patient young women, who never get exasperated – no matter how many times you change your mind – this is a small haven for quirky and well-made accessories such as bags, jewellery and belts. It's obvious everything's been chosen with great care, which is refreshing.
✉ **Calle del Barquillo 31, Chueca** ☎ **91 308 12 80** Ⓜ **Chueca** ⏲ **Mon-Sat 10am-2pm & 5-9pm**

Piamonte (3, C14)
Even repressed women have been known to climax at the sight of so many fantastic handbags, available in all shapes and sizes and in any colour you care to mention. There's a great range of jewellery on offer too, as well as a judicious selection of just-so shoes that will go perfectly with the bag.
✉ **Calle de Piamonte 16, Chueca** ☎ **91 522 45 80** Ⓜ **Chueca** ⏲ **Mon-Sat 10.30am-2pm & 5-8.30pm**

Sephora (3, G10)

Feeling less than fragrant? Or looking for a mother lode of make-up? Sephora is a smartly black-and-white kitted-out store with all the big cosmetic ranges and what seems like 1000 smells.

✉ **Puerta del Sol 3, Sol** ☎ **91 523 71 71** Ⓜ **Sol** ◷ **Mon-Sat 10am-9pm**

Women' Secret

(2, K7) Hankering to be taken for a madrileña? Then you'll have to start with the basics. Spanish women love their scanties, and this groovy, up-to-the-minute store (part of a chain) has plenty, plus swimwear.

✉ **Calle de Velázquez 48, Salamanca** ☎ **91 578 14 53** Ⓜ **Velázquez** ◷ **Mon-Sat 10am-8.30pm**

shhhh - Women' Secret

MARKETS

Mercadillo Marqués de Viana (2, C5)

A less touristy flea market than El Rastro is this Sunday morning shopping fest, held in and around the street of the same name in the Tetuán *barrio*. You'll find fresh produce, second-hand clothes and stacks of fun junk.

✉ **Calle de Marqués de Viana, Tetuán** Ⓜ **Tetuán** ◷ **Sun & hols 9am-2pm**

Mercadillo Plaza de las Comendadores

(3, A7) Madrid's markets usually take place in the morning to early afternoon, but this one allows the night-owl to get among it and sort through some trash and treasure. There are plenty of handicrafts of varying quality.

✉ **Plaza de las Comendadores, Malasaña** Ⓜ **Noviciados** ◷ **Sat 6-10pm**

Mercadillo de Sellos y Monedas (3, G8)

Every Sunday sees Madrid's coin and stamp sellers hawk their wares to Madrid's coin and stamp collectors. Start your day with a coffee in the plaza and check out a slice of local life.

✉ **Plaza Mayor, Los Austrias** Ⓜ **Sol** ◷ **Sun & hols 9am-2pm**

Mercado de San Miguel (3, H7)

If you're self-catering, then this is the market for you. This place, which is quite small, is not a bad spot to seek out fresh fruit and vegetables. It's also a good place to pick-up a quick lunch or just have a look at some rather attractive produce. If you're not hungry or not planning to shop, the building itself, a well-restored wrought-iron structure is worth checking out – even if it's closed.

✉ **Plaza de San Miguel, Los Austrias** Ⓜ **Sol** ◷ **Mon-Fri 9am-2.30pm & 5.15-8.15pm, Sat 9am-2.30pm**

MUSIC

El Flamenco Vive
(3, G6) Flamenco aficionados and novices alike take note: this store devotes itself to the subject of flamenco dance and music. There are books, CDs, instruments and costumes.
✉ **Calle de Conde de Lemos 7, Los Austrias** ☎ **91 547 39 17** e www.elflamenco vive.com Ⓜ **Ópera** ◷ **Mon-Sat 10.30am-2pm & 5-9pm**

El Real Musical
(3, F6) Its location near the Teatro Real should be a giveaway as to what kind of musical tastes are catered for here. Yep, it's classical all the way, with sheet music, CDs, books and instruments temptingly arranged.
✉ **Calle de Carlos III 1, Los Austrias** ☎ **91 541 30 07** Ⓜ **Sol** ◷ **Mon-Sat 10am-2.15pm & 4.30-8pm**

Garrido-Bailén
(3, H5) If Spain has inspired you to take up an instrument, or you're looking to upgrade your

existing one, then this shop will please you – it has just about every kind of instrument, plus sheet music and other musical sundries.
✉ **Calle Mayor 88, Los Austrias** ☎ **91 542 45 01** Ⓜ **Ópera** ◷ **Mon-Fri 10am-1.30pm & 4.30-8pm, Sat 10am-1.45pm**

Loud Vinyl (3, A10)
Perhaps you already have a vinyl addiction. Perhaps Madrid's DJs have turned you on to nonstop beats. Either way, Loud Vinyl can help, with European and US releases, and not a CD in sight.
✉ **Calle de Velarde 16, Malasaña** ☎ **91 446 41 92** Ⓜ **Tribunal** ◷ **Mon-Sat 10am-2.30pm & 5-9pm**

Madrid Rock (3, E10)
There's a good selection of music in this store. There's also the added bonus that you can purchase concert tickets here too. Cash only is accepted for ticket purchases. And if you can't get here, there's also a second branch, known as

MR Overstock, at Calle de San Martín 3.
✉ **Gran Vía 25, Gran Vía** ☎ **91 521 02 39** Ⓜ **Gran Vía** ◷ **10am-10pm**

Tipo (3, E10)
This hip and happening Malasaña/Chueca record store sells CDs and T-shirts as well as hosting CD signing sessions by performers.
✉ **Calle de Fuencarral 4, Gran Vía** ☎ **902 10 38 21** Ⓜ **Gran Vía** ◷ **Mon-Sat 10am-2pm & 5-8pm**

Garrido-Bailén

SPECIALIST STORES

Amantis (3, C12)
With a wide variety of lubricants, condoms, underwear, games, books and penisy things, Amantis is a popular sex shop with the gay crowd of Chueca and the brown-paper-bag brigade.
✉ **Calle de Pelayo 46, Chueca** ☎ **91 702 05 10** Ⓜ **Chueca** ◷ **Mon-Sat 11am-10pm, Sun 6-10pm**

Capas de Seseña
(3, G10) Madrid's winter will get you in the mood to rug up, and this shop will make nothing less than the best seem a necessity. The capes here are beautifully made and, despite Esquillace's 1766 attempt to make capes (at least long ones) illegal in Madrid, you'll attract nothing but envious glances if

you don one. Even Hillary Clinton bought one from here.
✉ **Calle de la Cruz 23, Huertas** ☎ **91 531 68 40** Ⓜ **Sol** ◷ **Mon-Fri 10am-2pm & 4.30-8pm, Sat 10am-2pm**

Casa Exerez (4, J9)
Get those shoes you've been punishing repaired here. This a curious, old-

how to use this book

SYMBOLS

- ✉ address
- ☎ telephone number
- Ⓜ nearest metro station
- Ⓡ nearest Cercanía station
- 🚌 nearest bus route
- ◷ opening hours
- ① tourist information
- ⑤ cost, entry charge
- ⓔ email/website address
- ♿ wheelchair access
- ⚕ child-friendly
- ✕ on-site or nearby eatery
- Ⓥ good vegetarian selection

COLOUR-CODING

Each chapter has a different colour code which is reflected on the maps for quick reference (eg all Highlights are bright yellow on the maps).

MAPS

The fold-out maps inside the front and back covers are numbered from 1 to 4. All sights and venues in the text have map references which indicate where to find them on the maps; eg, (3, E14) means Map 3, grid reference E14. Although every item is not pin-pointed on the maps, the street address is always indicated.

PRICES

Price gradings (eg $10/5) usually indicate adult/concession entry charges to a venue. Concession prices can include senior, student, member or coupon discounts.

AUTHOR AUTHOR!

Sally O'Brien

Sally first visited Madrid in the '80s as a teen, where she was intrigued by *la movida*, the excellent shoe shopping, the art and the fact that a singing nun forced wine on her during Midnight Mass. An impecunious summer in Madrid in the '90s led to an even greater appreciation of beer, tapas and museum air-conditioning. In the '00s, she sees no reason to change the way she conducts herself, except to take a notebook.

Muchas Gracias: Diana, Gabrielle, Charles, Katrina, Heather, Simone and Steven at LP; Damien Simonis; Martin Hughes – for Condensed advice; Fabi, Marie-Claire, Zoe, Jaime, Janine, Anthony, Marina, Paola and María; Lara, Jody and Gerard.

READER FEEDBACK

Things change – prices go up, schedules change, good places go bad and bad places improve or go bankrupt. So, if you find things better or worse, recently opened or long since closed, please tell us and help make the next edition even more accurate. Send all correspondence to the Lonely Planet office closest to you (listed on page 2) or visit ⓔ www.lonelyplanet.com/feedback.

Lonely Planet books provide independent advice. Lonely Planet does not accept advertising in guidebooks, nor payment in exchange for listing or endorsing any place or business. Lonely Planet writers do not accept discounts or payments in exchange for positive coverage of any sort.

world throwback on a street known for five-star fashion.
✉ **Calle Jose Ortega y Gasset 11, Salamanca** ☎ 91 431 63 07 Ⓜ **Núñez de Balboa** 🕐 Mon-Sat 10am-1.30pm

Casa Jiménez (3, E9)
It's easy to fall under the spell of Madrid's beautiful embroidered *mantones* (shawls), and even easier to succumb if you wander into this shop, which specialises in these as well as lace wraps.
✉ **Calle de Preciados 42, Sol** ☎ 91 548 05 26 Ⓜ **Sol or Callao** 🕐 Mon-Sat 10am-1.30pm & 5-8pm

El Templo de Fútbol (3, E9) For those who eat, sleep and breathe football, and have the appropriate outfit for it. On offer are strips from many clubs, footy boots and some gear from other sports thrown in for good measure.
✉ **Gran Vía 38, Gran Vía** ☎ 91 701 02 41 Ⓜ **Callao** 🕐 Mon-Sat 10am-9pm

La Cuenta (3, D13)
A tiny, stark-white box with hundreds of different types of beads displayed in jars, this shop gets filled to the brim with crafty types looking to make their own jewellery, and parents looking to occupy their children. Books on making beaded jewellery are also available.
✉ **Calle del Almirante 6, Chueca** ☎ 91 524 01 26 Ⓜ **Chueca** 🚈 **Recoletos** 🕐 Mon-Sat 11am-2pm & 5.30-9pm

Loewe (2, L6)
If you're *really* into leather and like combining it with the high end of things, Loewe's your store. With a long-standing international reputation for buttery soft bags, wallets, belts and some seriously elegant fashions, you need never be out of leather if your heart so desires.
✉ **Calle de Serrano 26 (men's at No 34), Salamanca** ☎ 91 426 35 88 Ⓜ **Serrano** 🕐 Mon-Sat 9.30am-8.30pm

Marihuana (3, K8)
Forgotten to pack your bong? Then Marihuana may be of help. Packed to the gills with smokers' requisites (mostly of the dope-smoking variety) and rock T-shirts, it attracts big crowds when El Rastro's on – and complaints of industrial deafness.
✉ **Plaza de Cascorro 6, La Latina** ☎ 91 467 35 92 Ⓜ **La Latina** 🕐 Mon-Sat 10am-2pm & 5-8.30pm, Sun 10am-2pm

Maty (3, F9)
Everything you could ever need to flamenco can be found here, from heels and ruffled dresses to performance videos for inspiration, as well as information on classes. It's not a bad spot

Going Dotty?
If you're in Madrid during any of the fiestas that see madrileños don their finest traditional gear, you may develop a taste for a ruffled polka-dot dress, colourful shawls or black-and-white check caps. The area around Plaza Mayor is a good (if a little touristy) source of such gear, but our faves have also include **Maty** (p71) and **Casa Jiménez** (p71). The less extravagant may simply want to tuck a carnation behind an ear.

for fellas to pick up some check caps either.
✉ **Calle de Maestro Victoria 2, Sol** ☎ 91 531 32 91 Ⓜ **Sol** 🕐 Mon-Fri 10am-1.45pm & 5-8.30pm, Sat 10am-2pm & 5-8pm

Sobrinos de Perez (3, G9) This shop can supply you with everything your sacred heart may desire. Everything's got a Catholic edge. If you're looking for kitsch, don't make it too obvious.
✉ **Calle de Postas 6, Los Austrias** Ⓜ **Sol** 🕐 Mon-Sat 9.45am-2pm & 4.30-8pm

Have you got one in pink? Sobrinos de Perez

places to eat

It's only fitting that Madrid, at the centre of Spain, should offer a distillation of Spanish cuisine of all types. This is thanks to its status as a city of Spanish immigrants bringing with them Asturian, Andalucian, Basque, Navarran, Catalan, Valencian, Murcian and Galician (among others) cooking styles. It also offers some great international cuisines, with French, Mediterranean, Japanese, Thai, Indian, Kurdish, Mexican and North African widely available. Perhaps most surprisingly, Madrid is a great spot for seafood, with ocean catches transported daily to the capital for the hungry hordes!

Grazers will love the ritual of the tapas crawl and sampling titbits in such a social way. Big eaters will love the long, hearty lunches washed down with wine and punctuated by animated conversation.

MENÚ DEL DÍA

Every restaurant in Madrid will have (by law) its version of the *menú del día* – a set-lunch menu offering three courses and a drink. They cost about half as much as three courses and a drink from the á la carte menu, and are a great way to refuel Madrid-style (over about three hours!) for a reasonable price.

Meal Costs
The pricing symbols used in this chapter indicate the cost of a three-course meal with a drink. For tapas joints, it's two portions and a drink.

$	under €10
$$	€11-20
$$$	€21-35
$$$$	over €36

DINING HOURS & BOOKING

Madrileños love to eat and they love to eat late! Most of them will have three or four courses for lunch (*never* before 2pm, and that will generally last until 4pm), and no-one will even consider dinner before 10pm. Get into the rhythm of the city's dining habits and you'll have a lot more fun.

A lot of places close on Sunday (and public holidays) and quite a few places close for part of August – or all of it. Still, there's no reason to think you'll starve. Because dining out is so popular here, you'd be well advised to make reservations for more expensive restaurants, especially at weekends or for lunch. Credit cards are widely accepted, although inexpensive restaurants generally accept cash only.

Madrid's Cuisine

Frankly, it's a good thing that Madrid is filled with dining options from the rest of Spain, as most home-grown cuisine is a little bland for many tastes. Local staples include **cocido a la madrileña** (see Madrid's Dullest Dish p83) and **callos a la madrileña**, which is tripe casserole with chorizo and chillies. You might also sample **sopa de ajo** (garlic soup) or **sopa castellana**, which is a basic broth with an egg floating in it. Hardly inspiring stuff – but if it's inspiration you seek…

Tapas will provide you with some of your fondest memories of Madrid. Don't go messing with the word and thinking it's a strict definition, with certain requisite ingredients. Tapas are not just things you eat – they are a way of eating, and therefore a way of socialising and forging (or reinforcing) relationships.

The word itself means lid, or top. The verb form, *tapar*, means to top or to cover, and most people believe that the origin of tapas was in the 18th century, when tavern keepers would place a slice of ham or bread on the mouth of a glass to keep the flies out. It's also the best way of soaking up alcohol on a night out!

You'll find tapas in almost every bar in Madrid (larger portions are known as *raciones*). A few of the most common nibbling options (apart from olives, which you generally receive as par for the course) include:

albóndigas	meatballs
bacalao	cod
boquerones	fresh anchovies marinated in wine vinegar
callos	tripe
chorizo	spicy red cooked sausage
gambas al ajillo	prawns cooked in garlic-laden olive oil
jamón	ham
morcilla	blood sausage (fried)
pulpo gallego	spicy boiled octopus
tortilla española	potato & onion omelette

ARGÜELLES

Cañas y Tapas
(2, G2)   **$**
Tapas
Part of a newish (since 1999) chain specialising in tapas (although full meals are also available), these places are handy ports of call when fatigue and famine get the better of you. They are all over Madrid, and the San Miguel flows freely. Don't worry, locals are happy to come here too.
✉ **Calle de la Princesa 76** ☎ **902 18 09 18** Ⓜ **Moncloa** ⏰ **1.30-4.30pm & 9pm-midnight** ⚇

Casa Mingo
(2, L1)   **$**
Asturian
Casa Mingo likes to keep things simple: chicken and cider, the Asturian way. It's a cheery, cheap and chipper place to enjoy a hearty lunch, with a bit of history thrown in, as this place has been cidering up beside madrileños since 1888.
✉ **Paseo de la Florida 34** ☎ **91 547 79 18** Ⓜ **Príncipe Pío** ⏰ **11am-midnight**

El Molino de los Porches
(3, B3)   **$$$$**
Castilian
Roasted meat and fish dishes predominate here, and it does a busy trade, especially when the weather's good, as this means the verdant *terraza* – with Casa de Campo in sight – can be put to good use.
✉ **Paseo del Pintor Rosales 1** ☎ **91 548 13 36** Ⓜ **Ventura**

Rodríguez
⏰ **noon-4.30pm & 8pm-midnight** ⚇

La Vaca Argentina
(2, K1)   **$$$**
Argentinian
Make an enormous deposit in your body's iron bank right here. Slabs of Argentinian meat are the speciality (washed down with Argentinian wine), and while the cowhide walls are verging on overkill, this place is very popular, with numerous branches throughout the city. Try to get yourself a seat outside.
✉ **Paseo del Pintor Rosales 52** ☎ **91 559 66 05** Ⓜ **Argüelles** ⏰ **1-4.30pm & 9pm-12.30am**

Diet Dilemmas
Being a vegetarian isn't too difficult in Madrid, although being a vegan will present problems. However, spare a thought for those wanting to keep kosher. Spain expelled its Jews in 1492 and you'd still think that Isabel and Ferdinand were in charge if you scanned many menus: pork and shellfish as far as the eye can see.

CHAMBERÍ

Combarro
(4, A6) $$$
Galician
Combarro offers its diners quality Galician seafood, especially *pulpo* (octopus). It's not a fancy place, but it's popular with business-men and women on a lunchbreak, so you may have a bit of a wait, which is the perfect excuse to prop up the bar and imbibe, nibble and chat.
✉ **Calle de la Reina Mercedes 12** ☎ **91 554 77 84** Ⓜ **Alvarado** ⏰ 1.30-4pm & Mon-Sat 8pm-midnight

El Bodegon
(4, G9) $$$$
Basque
El Bodegon has a strong reputation for excellent Basque cooking and old-fashioned service. Try the *rodaballo* (turbot) if it's on the menu – the traditional approach doesn't mean the chef's afraid to try new ingredients and techniques.
✉ **Calle del Pinar 15** ☎ **91 562 31 37** Ⓜ **Gregorio Marañón** ⏰ Mon-Fri 1-4pm & 8pm-midnight, Sat 8pm-midnight

El Doble (4, F5) $$
Tapas
Judging by the photos, this busy tapas bar is owned by bullfighting enthusiasts. The tapas and *raciones* are very good – try the *ventresca* (meat from around the stomach of a tuna). Don't panic if you get drunk and think you're seeing double; there are two of these bars on this street with the same name.
✉ **Calle de Ponzano 58** ☎ **91 441 47 18**

Jai Alai (before the hungry hordes arrive)

Ⓜ **Alonso Cano** ⏰ Mon-Sat 11am-3pm & 6pm-midnight

Jai Alai
(4, B9) $$$
Basque
Every second person will tell you that Basque cook-ing is the country's best, and this long-running place (with a curious English look to the decor) will often get a mention in the next breath. Among other things, the pork dishes are handled beautifully and service is sterling.
✉ **Calle Balbina Valverde 2** ☎ **91 561 27 42** Ⓜ **Nuevos**

Ministerios ⏰ Tues-Sun 1-4pm & 9pm-midnight ♿

Santceloni
(4, F8) $$$$
Market
This smartly decorated yet comfortable restaurant is in the basement of the Hesperia Hotel. It's the sort of place that chefs, food writers and enthusiasts put ahead of anything else on their 'must do' list for Madrid. Superlatives just don't cut it; suffice to say that chef Santi Santamaría should be made the patron saint of exquisite food. You'd be well advised to

---

Vegetarian Options

Madrid loves its meat, but there are plenty of places to tuck into vegetarian food. Try: **Chez Pomme** (p76), **La Bio Tika** (p80), **El Estragón** (pp81–2), **Isla de Tesoro** (p84) and **Artemisa** (p87) for strictly vegetarian dining. For restaurants with good vegie options, look at: **El Pepinillo de Barquillo** (p76), **Wokcafe** (p78), **El Cenador del Prado** (pp79–80), **La Finca de Susanna** (p80), **La Tentación de San Miguel** (p83), **Mumbai Massala** (p86) and **Thai Gardens** (pp86–7). The Ⓥ indicates that a place is either full vegetarian or has an excellent selection of vegetarian dishes.

make a lunch or dinner reservation.
✉ **Hesperia Hotel, Paseo de la Castellana 57** ☎ **91 210 88 40** Ⓜ **Gregorio Marañón** ◷ Mon-Fri 2-4pm & 9-11pm, Sat 9-11pm

Santo Mauro
(4, J7) **$$$$**
Basque
If you're staying here, you'll find it hard to leave, so it's fortunate that the restaurant, housed in the former library, is a delight. We

enjoyed both the *bacalao* (cod) and the garden view.
✉ **Calle de Zurbano 36** ☎ **91 319 69 00** Ⓜ **Rubén Darío or Alonso Martínez** ◷ noon-4pm & 8pm-midnight ♿

CHUECA

Baires Café
(3, C12) **$$**
Café
Airy, full of light and not a bad spot to refresh yourself with some caffeine (or something stronger) after some busy times in Chueca, this place appeals because the atmosphere's cool but easy-going, and exhibitions or DJs may get thrown into the bargain.
✉ **Calle de Gravina 4** ☎ **91 532 98 79** Ⓜ **Chueca** ◷ Mon-Sat 11am-2am

---

Market Cuisine
Many restaurants listed in this chapter specialise in 'market cuisine', which means that the day's menu is based on what looked good at the market that morning, rather than a particular style of cooking or category of cuisine.

Café Miranda
(3, C13) **$$$**
Theatre restaurant
It's a cliché to say that gay places do wonderful things with flowers and lighting, and this place reinforces it. Stunningly attractive, with lovingly presented, well-prepared dishes – and probably the easiest and

most enjoyable way to catch a really good drag act. Reservations advised.
✉ **Calle del Barquillo 29** ☎ **91 521 29 46** Ⓜ **Chueca** ◷ 9pm-1am

Chez Pomme
(3, D11) **$$**
Vegetarian
A smart-looking place, with a loyal clientele from the gay community, Chez Pomme serves up tasty vegetarian morsels and substantial mains, all without ramming earth-tones down your throat, like so many healthy places. The *menú del día* is excellent value.
✉ **Calle de Pelayo 4** ☎ **91 531 57 73** Ⓜ **Chueca** ◷ Mon-Sat 1.30-4.30pm & 8.30-11.30pm Ⓥ

El Pepinillo de Barquillo
(3, C13) **$$$**
Creative
Humorous touches (such as the giant gherkin hanging from the ceiling) don't detract from the seriously good food, which combines fresh ingredients with some interesting ideas. Apparently, this place is good for star-spotting the odd celebrity but we think it's Ángela, the chef, who's the star.
✉ **Calle del Barquillo 42** ☎ **91 310 25 46**

Ⓜ **Chueca** ◷ 1-5pm & 8.30pm-2am Ⓥ

La Barraca
(3, E12) **$$$**
Paella/Valencian
This is an extremely popular spot for locals and visitors, partly because of its inviting atmosphere, with low whitewashed timber rafters, but mostly because it serves up hearty, flavoursome paellas. Try to get in early (before 2pm or 10pm).
✉ **Calle de la Reina 29** ☎ **91 532 71 54** Ⓜ **Gran Vía or Banco de España** ◷ 1-4pm & 8.30pm-midnight ♿

La Buena Vida
(3, C14) **$$**
Market
This very smart-looking restaurant features some good modern art on the walls, open spaces and swish bathrooms, and keeps its menu fairly straightforward. Dishes are perfect for a lightish lunch and there's a good bar.
✉ **Calle Conde de Xiquena 8** ☎ **91 531 31 49** Ⓜ **Chueca** 🚊 **Recoletos** ◷ Mon-Sat 1.30-4pm & 9pm-midnight

La Dame Noire
(3, C11) **$$$**
French
This lavish, theatrically decorated restaurant (think

flock wallpaper, gilt and candlelight) specialises in wonderfully rich French food (consult your friendly cardiologist if in doubt) and assiduously cultivated service. Oh, and there's a drag-queen floorshow on Thursday. Reservations are recommended.

✉ **Calle de Perez Galdós 3** ☎ **91 531 04 76** Ⓜ **Chueca** or **Tribunal** ⊕ **Tues-Thur & Sun 9pm-1am, Fri & Sat 9pm-2.30am**

La Gastroteca de Stéphane y Arturo
(3, D12) **$$$$**
Creative
The 1980s was the decade to come up with some crazy eating ideas, and this place is the spiritual home of Madrid's 'creative' cuisine scene. Specialities include all sorts of things you probably never thought you would eat. For example, the *raya de mantequilla* (stingray). For some diners, things may seem 'out there' just for the sake of it.

✉ **Plaza de Chueca 8** ☎ **91 532 25 64** Ⓜ **Chueca** ⊕ **Mon-Fri 1-3.30pm & 9-11.30pm, Sat 9-11.30pm**

La Panza es Primero
(3, D12) **$$**
Mexican
Admire the Mexi-kitsch and get yourself settled with a Coronita (or perhaps a tequila) and a plump south-of-the-border taco. Service is friendly and fast, and the tacos are good for kids, as they can be ordered one at a time, with a range of fillings.

✉ **Calle de la Libertad 33** ☎ **91 521 76 40** Ⓜ **Chueca** ⊕ **1pm-1am** ♣

La Sastrería
(3, C12) **$**
Café
Whether you're getting in a post-boogie breakfast or kick-starting the night, you'll find plenty of like-minded folks at this popular Chueca hang-out. The name means 'dressmaker' in Spanish, and various decor odds-and-ends reflect this – some of the customers look as though they've come straight from a fitting too.

✉ **Calle de Hortaleza 74** ☎ **91 532 07 71** Ⓜ **Chueca** ⊕ **10am-2.30pm**

Lombok
(3, D12) **$$$**
Creative
Lombok was an 'in' destination when we visited, making it tricky to procure a table at times. The restaurant has a lot of white going on, creating an airy, sometimes chilly feel, especially with the stainless steel tables. The food is great though –

fresh and imaginatively prepared.

✉ **Calle de Augusto Figueroa 32** ☎ **91 531 35 66** Ⓜ **Chueca** ⊕ **Mon-Thur 2-4pm & 9pm-midnight, Fri & Sat 9pm-1am**

madrilia
(3, E11) **$$$**
Mediterranean
The lower-case 'm' should give you a fairly good idea of what you can expect from this place. Modern, creative dishes (the rice dishes are recommended) are served up in slick, blue-lit surrounds to a smart yet hungry set. Reservations for weekend dining are a good idea.

✉ **Calle de Clavel 6** ☎ **91 523 92 75** Ⓜ **Gran Vía** ⊕ **1-4pm & 8.30pm-midnight**

Stop Madrid
(3, D11) **$**
Tapas
Stop Madrid from what? Gorging on delicious tapas? Not likely. This

Stop by Stop Madrid

popular local spot gets busy in the afternoon and evening, and has some great wines. There are plenty of yellowing tiles, lots of dark wood and very warm service. Tapas is mostly *jamón-* and *chorizo*-based.

✉ Calle Hortaleza 11
☎ 91 523 54 42

Ⓜ Gran Via ⏲ Mon-Sat 12.30-4pm & 6pm-2am

Wokcafe
(3, E12) $$$
Asian
Chueca's always happy to embrace the new, and Wokcafe has proved popular for its quality stir-fries.

There's also a shop, and a bar for coffee or cocktails. The Asian-inspired decor avoids sterility thanks to the triffid-style greenery and beaten-gold wall.

✉ Calle de las Infantas 44 ☎ 91 522 90 69
Ⓜ Banco de España
⏲ Mon-Sat 10am-2am
♿ Ⓥ

HUERTAS & SANTA ANA

Asia Society
(3, H13) $$$
Asian
The tiles and blonde wood hail from the world of New York-Pacific Rim fusion, not classic Madrid. Dishes come from Thailand, Korea, Japan and Indonesia, and a lot of groovy madrileños tuck in, even at the early hour of 10pm! The green mango salad was a piece of tangy, textural heaven. Book at weekends.

✉ Calle Lope de Vega 37 ☎ 91 429 92 92
Ⓜ Antón Martín
⏲ Tues-Sat 1-4pm & 9pm-12.30am

Café del Círculo de Bellas Artes
(3, F13) $$
Café/Brasserie
This cavernous *belle époque* (1919) space is marvellous for a caffeine or champagne hit, or a meal while resting weary feet and sussing out the well-dressed patrons from the terrace. To gain access, you'll need a temporary membership token (60c). Definitely the best spot to revel in the monumental architecture of the surrounding area.

✉ Calle de Alcalá 42
☎ 91 531 85 03

Ⓜ Banco de España
⏲ Mon-Thur & Sun 9am-2am, Fri & Sat 9am-3am

Café del Príncipe
(3, G11) $
Café
Although it stays open till late, we prefer this place in the morning when you can sit at a window seat, sip a coffee and watch Madrid go by. It's a nice mix of chandeliers, unhurried smiles and a fruit-pokie machine.

✉ Plaza de Canelejas 5 ☎ 91 531 93 84
Ⓜ Sevilla ⏲ 9am-3am

Eat & Run
Two mobile food options in Madrid are the *barquillo-* (wafer) selling *castizos* who frequent the Parque del Buen Retiro on weekends with their red barrels, and the Chinese hawkers plying ready-made *boccadillos* or simple rice dishes on Gran Vía or around Huertas late at night. The former is a local tradition, the latter attracts the attention of police.

The society of great food

Casa Alberto
(3, H11) **$**
Tapas
With pics, paintings and tiles on the walls plus fancy woodwork, this place is a great spot to nibble tapas while quenching a beer or *vermut* (vermouth) thirst. Service is courteous and you can eat in the restaurant ($$) at the back if you hanker for something more substantial.
✉ **Calle de las Huertas 18 ☎ 91 429 93 56**
Ⓜ **Antón Martín**
🕐 **Tuesday-Sunday noon-5.30pm & 8pm-1.30am**

Cervecería Alemana
(3, H11) **$$**
Tapas
A definite stop on the Hemingway pilgrimage, the tapas and beers here attract many tourists at night, but it retains a local feel during the day. Tables have marble tops and there's a lot of brown going on.
✉ **Plaza de Santa Ana 6 ☎ 91 429 70 33**
Ⓜ **Antón Martín or Sol**
🕐 **Mon, Wed, Thur & Sun 10.30am-1am, Fri & Sat 10.30am-2am**

Champagnería Gala
(3, J13) **$$$**
Paella/Valencian
Make a reservation for this place as soon as you arrive in Madrid. Even so, you might not get a table until about 4pm for lunch, but the rich paella, glass-covered atrium, friendly service and general conviviality of everyone around you make it worth the wait. Credit cards are not accepted.
✉ **Calle de Moratín 22 ☎ 91 420 19 50**

Swill a cerveza at Casa Alberto

Ⓜ **Antón Martín**
🕐 **2-5pm & 9pm-1.30am ♿**

Donzoko
(3, G11) **$$$**
Japanese
If Spain's (at times) heavy cuisine is holding you back, head for a sushi fix at this popular place with Japanese staples (right down to the tiny Zen-like rock-garden entrance) that are popular with locals and tourists.
✉ **Calle Echegaray 3 ☎ 91 429 57 20**
Ⓜ **Sevilla** 🕐 **Mon-Sat 1.30-3.30pm & 8.30-11.30pm ♿**

East 47 (3, G12) **$$$$**
Creative
Both a restaurant and a stylish bar, this reflects its parent, the Hotel Villa Real, as it has a feeling of luxury without being predictable. The meat dishes are particularly strong, and the wine list is worth exploring.
✉ **Hotel Villa Real, Plaza de las Cortes 10 ☎ 91 420 37 67**
Ⓜ **Banco de España**
🕐 **11am-1am**

El Caldero
(3, H11) **$$**
Murcian
All muted earth-tones and cuisine from Murcia, this place does a wicked line of rice-based dishes for two. The *dorada a la sal* (rock-salt crusted Dory – €13.25) or *arroz negro* (rice with squid ink – €20) are excellent choices, but attentive staff will help the indecisive.
✉ **Calle de las Huertas 15 ☎ 91 429 50 44**
Ⓜ **Antón Martín**
🕐 **Tues-Sat 1.30-4pm & 9pm-midnight, Mon & Sun 1.30-4pm**

El Cenador del Prado
(3, H11) **$$$**
Creative
When your eyes get used to the riot of red, purple and pink near the

Want Smoke With That?
The campaigns against smoking that are par for the course in many countries have had little impact here. In fact, it would seem that most madrileños have a cigarette 'twixt their lips 24 hours a day, only removing them to take a sip or a mouthful of food. Some restaurants have designated no-smoking areas, but these are rarities.

entrance, you'll probably get taken to a cool, light-filled atrium, where exceptionally prescient service awaits, along with a wonderful modern menu and some of the most lavish desserts we've ever seen.
✉ **Calle del Prado 4**
☎ **91 429 15 61**
Ⓜ **Antón Martín or Sol**
🕙 **Mon-Fri 1.30-4pm & 9pm-midnight, Sat 9pm-midnight** **V**

La Bio Tika
(3, J12)   **$**
Vegetarian
Feeling that your food pyramid's been turned upside-down? Try here – the healthy (and flavoursome) cuisine is vegetarian *and* macrobiotic, service is calm and casual, and the no-smoking policy is a bonus.
✉ **Calle Amor de Dios 3** ☎ **91 429 07 80**
Ⓜ **Antón Martín**
🕙 **Mon-Fri 1-4.30pm & 8-11.30pm; Sat, Sun & public hols 1.30-4.30pm** **V**

La Dolores
(3, H13)   **$**
Tapas
Great tilework out the front (since 1907) and an ear-splitting crowd inside – an excellent place to refresh yourself once you've done the museum

trawl. While the tapas are very good, a 'world of beer' theme seems to be taking place on the shelves, which is *so* 80s.
✉ **Plaza de Jesús 4**
☎ **91 429 22 43**
Ⓜ **Antón Martín**
🕙 **Mon-Thur & Sun 11am-1am, Fri & Sat 11am-2am**

La Fábrica
(3, J13)   **$**
Tapas
Close to the Prado and the jumping Santa Ana night-time playground (without the pesky tourist trade), this bar has great tapas (the canapés are from heaven) and a convivial, chatty atmosphere that's hard to beat. There's also room to sit down and take the weight off those aching feet out the back.
✉ **Calle de Jesús 2**
☎ **91 369 06 71**
Ⓜ **Antón Martín**
🕙 **Mon-Thur 11am-1am, Fri & Sat 11am-2am**

La Farfalla
(3, J12)   **$$**
Italian/Argentinian
La Farfalla may not have the greatest Italian food you'll ever have, but the pasta dishes are filling and the steaks are more than substantial. We figure the place's best assets are the

friendliness and very long opening hours!
✉ **Calle de Santa María 17** ☎ **91 369 46 91** Ⓜ **Antón Martín**
🕙 **9pm-3am** ♿ **V**

La Finca de Susanna
(3, G11)   **$$**
Mediterranean
Incredible value, given the modern, attractive decor and imaginative dishes, but this place is no secret. Get in early, or join a long queue. The *menú del día* is extraordinary for €6.60, but off-the-menu ordering will deliver the same happy surprise.
✉ **Calle de Arlabán 4**
☎ **91 369 35 57**
Ⓜ **Sevilla** 🕙 **1-3.45pm & 8.30-11.45pm** **V**

Los Gatos
(3, J13)   **$**
Tapas
Like a mission-brown explosion in a bullfighting-kitsch factory, this place brings new meaning to the phrase 'cheek by jowl'. If you're lucky, you'll see the overworked grill on fire when tapas overload occurs. A definite fave, especially the *anguilas* (little eels on toast).
✉ **Calle de Jesús 2**
☎ **91 429 30 67**
Ⓜ **Antón Martín**
🕙 **Mon-Thur & Sun noon-1am, Fri & Sat noon-2am**

La Trucha
(3, G10)   **$**
Tapas
This is one of Madrid's best spots for tapas, especially if it's Andalucian that you're after. The seafood nibbles are truly scrumptious, but you can also eat out the back if you're after something more substantial.
✉ **Calle de Manuel Fernández y González 3**

Los Gatos – a firm favourite

☎ 91 429 58 33 Ⓜ Sol or Sevilla ⏱ daily 1-4pm & 8pm-midnight

La Vaca Verónica (3, J13)   **$$**
Mediterranean
The ladies of La Vaca Verónica understand that good eating lies in the freshest, finest ingredients, simply prepared – our sardines were plump and juicy, and deserved their own postcode. The decor is yellow-hued, with a few chandeliers thrown in, although this little touch doesn't make it feel stuffy. Reservations are advised if you're planning to eat here at the weekend.
✉ **Calle Moratín 38**
☎ **91 429 78 27**

Cervecería Alemana, a nod to German beer-halls p79

Ⓜ **Antón Martín**
⏱ Mon-Sat noon-4pm & 9pm-midnight

Lhardy (3, G10)   **$$$$**
Tapas/French/Madrileña
A staple of swanky Madrid since 1839, this is the place to come for high-end tapas, French cuisine

– including the *perdiz estofado* (stuffed partridge) – and some excellent local dishes, including *callos* (tripe). The setting is impressive too.
✉ **Carrera de San Jerónimo 8** ☎ 91 522 22 07 Ⓜ Sol ⏱ Mon-Sat 1-3.30pm & 8.30-11.30pm, Sun 1-3.30pm

LA LATINA TO LAVAPIÉS

Asador Frontón (3, J9)   **$$$**
Basque
Nostrils and tastebuds start twitching with thoughts of this place, so good are the charcoal-grilled meat and fish dishes, and while the desserts may be too heavy after such

carnivorous festivities, the wine selection ensures you're getting more than just one food group – well, sorta.
✉ **Plaza Tirso de Molina 7** ☎ 91 369 16 17 Ⓜ Tirso de Molina ⏱ 1.30-4pm, Mon-Sat 9pm-midnight

Casa de Tostas (2, O5)   **$**
Tapas
Lavapiés residents know there's no point in socialising without getting stuck into *tostas*, and the ones here are pretty hefty. Generous serves, with a great range of toppings (the *pate de bacalao* is our favourite) and the place is full of a lot of happy munchers.
✉ **Calle de Argumosa 29** ☎ 91 527 08 42 Ⓜ Lavapiés ⏱ 1-4pm & 6pm-1am ♿

El Almendro 13 (3, J7)   **$**
Tapas
Don't get people started on the topic of the *huevos rotos* (scrambled eggs) here – they'll never stop. Just get started on the eggs themselves! Excellent tapas, a great atmosphere, and good wines make this place extremely popular.
✉ **Calle del Almendro 13** ☎ 91 365 42 52 Ⓜ La Latina ⏱ 1-4pm & 7pm-midnight ♿

El Estragón (3, J6)   **$$**
Vegetarian
With the pleasant Plaza de la Paja as a good spot to start off a social whirl, the mighty tasty food of this firm fave should see you sated. Staff are kind, even if you've shown up a little too late for their liking.
✉ **Plaza de la Paja 10** ☎ 91 365 89 82

Coffee Notes
Café con leche (drunk in the mornings only) is about half coffee, half hot milk. A *café solo* is a short black, while a *café cortado* is a short black with a dash of milk. For iced coffee, ask for a *café con hielo*, which will result in a glass of ice and a hot cup of coffee to be poured over the ice.

Focus on the food at Lamiak

🅜 **La Latina**
🕐 1.30-5pm & 8.30pm-midnight **V**

La Carpanta (3, J6) $
Tapas
One of the beauties of this place is that it's got more on offer than just beer and olives. The wines are carefully chosen and the canapés moreish. An even bigger bonus? There's room to sit too.
✉ **Calle de Almendro 22** ☎ **91 366 57 83**
🅜 **La Latina**
🕐 3pm-2am

Lamiak (3, J6) $
Tapas/Basque
There's also a great restaurant here ($$$), but it was the *pinchos* that left us breathless – they were Basque and they were simply great. The egg-yolk coloured walls had woeful art but who cares when the nibbles are this good and the beer is so expertly poured?
✉ **Calle de la Cava Baja 42** ☎ **91 365 52 12** 🅜 **La Latina**
🕐 Tues-Sat 1-4pm & 9pm-midnight, Sun 1-4pm

Tía Doly (2, O4) $$
Italian
Tía Doly (Aunt Doly) makes excellent fresh pasta on a daily basis and all in the homely surrounds of this unpretentious Italian restaurant. It's also possible to get meals to take away if you're staying nearby or fancy dining in the great outdoors.
✉ **Calle del Amparo 54** ☎ **91 527 33 26**
🅜 **Lavapiés** 🕐 Tues-Sat 8.30pm-12.30am, Wed-Sun 1-4.30pm

LOS AUSTRIAS

Casa Ciriaco (3, G6) $$
Castillian
A local eating place that's frequented by families, business folk, and amateur artists (look at the walls), the food here is unpretentious. Cluey waiters wear white jackets; they will even give your shirt a squirt of stain-remover if you've been sloppy with the *sopa di cocido* (€3.50).
✉ **Calle Mayor 84** ☎ **91 548 06 20**
🅜 **Ópera** 🕐 Thur-Tues 1.30-4.30pm & 8.30-11.30pm

Casa de Santa Cruz (3, H9) $$$
Market
This place certainly isn't lacking in atmosphere, as it's situated in the old Santa Cruz basilica. But you can relax, because despite the setting, it's short on both formality and stuffiness. The food is excellent market cuisine, and the lamb dishes we sampled bring new meaning to the phrase 'lamb of God'.
✉ **Calle de la Bolsa 12** ☎ **91 521 86 23**
🅜 **Sol** 🕐 1.30-4.30pm & 8.30pm-midnight

Casa Lucio (3, J7) $$$
Madrileña
Located on a street that's full of good places to eat, Casa Lucio remains a firm favourite for those who like to partake of well-prepared madrileña dishes, such as *arroz con leche* (rice pudding). The place is casual and welcoming, but can get busy, so you might have to stand at the bar for a while and wait for a table to be vacated.
✉ **Calle de la Cava Baja 35** ☎ **91 365 32 52** 🅜 **La Latina** 🕐 Sun-Fri 1-4pm, 9-11.30pm ♿

Casa Paco (3, H7) **$$$**
Madrileña
This charming old-style place specialises in madrileña cooking, and the meat and egg dishes come highly recommended. You're firmly in *castizo* territory here, so throw out the dietary restrictions and get busy loosening your belt.
✉ **Plaza de Puerta Cerrada 11** ☎ **91 366 31 66** Ⓜ **Sol** ◔ **Mon-Sat 1.30-4pm & 8.30pm-midnight** ♿

La Cruzada (3, F6) **$$**
Castillian
Not at its original 1827 address, but you'll be glad to know that the original sculpted wooden bar was brought along. This place is nothing flash, but the *raciones* are tasty and filling, and always a good idea as a substitute for 'children's portions'.
✉ **Calle de la Amnistía 8** ☎ **91 548 01 31** Ⓜ **Ópera** ◔ **Mon-Sat 1-4pm & 8.30pm-midnight** ♿

Las Bravas (3, G10) **$**
Tapas
Bravas specialises in *patatas bravas* (although the other tapas dishes are good too), so much so, that its sauce is patented (No 357492 if you're wondering). The decor is nothing to write home about, but the spuds certainly are!
✉ **Callejón de Álvarez Gato 3** Ⓜ **Sol** ◔ **noon-4.30pm & 8pm-midnight** ♿ **V**

La Tentación de San Miguel (3, H7) **$$$**
International
Housed in a sensitively renovated building just

Madrid's Dullest Dish?

Those looking for an 'authentic' dish from Madrid may well wish they'd stuck to all the other fine cuisine that's on offer. The most well-known local offering is *cocido a la madrileña*, a hearty stew that's said to be eaten 'from front to back'. Ingredients are generally chicken, chorizo, some ham (or other cured meat), potatoes, cabbage, chickpeas and macaroni (or rice). You start by eating the broth, with macaroni or rice. Then the chickpeas. Then the meat. By this stage, you'll have trouble fitting into your pants and walking at the same time. You'll also have trouble remembering why you ordered it, as a long cooking process often ensures that all flavour and texture have long disappeared. Still, locals love it and it certainly provides good winter fuel. On that level, we'll say it's not Madrid's dullest dish – we'll leave that honour to *churros*, those bland, greasy sticks of batter that require dunking to make them taste of anything.

near Plaza Mayor, this is a wonderful spot to sample a range of cuisines amid elegant, yet unfussy surrounds. We're fans of whatever they're doing to cous cous, but you can also pick up simple and high-quality tapas, while being surrounded by diners of all types.
✉ **Calle de Conde Miranda 4** ☎ **91 559 98 19** Ⓜ **Ópera** ◔ **noon-5pm & 8.30pm-1.30am** **V**

Posada de la Villa (3, J7) **$$$$**
Madrileña
A wonderfully restored 17th-century inn where all sorts of people, from travelling salesmen to fellows of ill repute were purported to have sought lodging. The food is classic madrileña, right down to the suckling pig.
✉ **Calle de la Cava Baja 9** ☎ **91 366 18 60** Ⓜ **La Latina** ◔ **1-4pm, Mon-Sat 8pm-midnight**

Restaurante Julián de Tolosa (3, J7) **$$$$**
Basque
A charmingly rustic atmosphere pervades this eatery – a Basque institution. Think lots of exposed brick and timber and solid batten-the-hatches food. Beans are a big feature on the menu, and if you want something to break up all that fibre, have a *chuletón* (enormous chop).
✉ **Calle de la Cava Baja 18** ☎ **91 365 82 10** Ⓜ **La Latina** ◔ **Mon-Sat 1-4.30pm & 8.30pm-midnight**

Restaurante Sobrino de Botín (3, H8) **$$$**
Castillian
We wonder if people even notice the food here, so busy are they soaking up all the history. Restaurante Sobrino is dubbed the oldest restaurant in the world. It's also featured in the well-known novels: Pérez

Galdós' *Fortunata y Jacinta* and Hemingway's *The Sun Also Rises*. Yep, you could say it's a bit of a tourist trap, but it's a good-looking trap all the same.

✉ **Calle de los Cuchillos 17** ☎ **91 366 42 17** Ⓜ **Sol or Tirso de Molina** ⏰ **1-4pm & 8pm-midnight** ♿

Taberna La Bola
(3, E6) **$$$$**
Madrileña
This *taberna* (tavern) is well known locally for its traditional *cocido a la madrileña*, and has been placating hungry madrileño tummies since 1880. There's a very nice old-fashioned atmosphere

here, with good old-fashioned service, and the high turnover means that you know you're getting the good, fresh stuff.

✉ **Calle de la Bola 5** ☎ **91 547 69 30** Ⓜ **Ópera or Santo Domingo** ⏰ **1.30-4pm, Mon-Sat 8.30pm-midnight** ♿

MALASAÑA & AROUND

Baban (4, K3) **$$**
Kurdish
Go downstairs once you've found Baban and feast on delicious dips and excellent meat dishes (best shared). It's a casual place, where locals come to have a relaxed meal in still-groovy surrounds (this is Malasaña after all).
✉ **Calle de Manuela Malasaña 20** ☎ **91 594 18 68** Ⓜ **San Bernardo or Bilbao** ⏰ **Tues-Sun 1-4pm & 9pm-midnight**

Bar Casa do Compañeiro
(3, B9) **$**
Tapas
The fried *morcilla* (black pudding) here is served with a few hunks of bread. It's plain and a bit stodgy but it certainly did the trick as a stomach liner-meets-iron deposit. It was good

Galician stuff too, and the smile we got warmed our hearts.
✉ **Calle de San Vicente Ferrer 44** ☎ **91 521 57 02** Ⓜ **Noviciado or Tribunal** ⏰ **1pm-2am**

Café Comercial
(4, K4) **$**
Café
A local institution of the best kind! The Café Comercial has been a meeting place, a *tertulia* (chat session) centre and breakfast spot for donkeys' years. Grab a coffee and a pastry or a snack, and people-watch from behind a newspaper. If the food's not enough, come for the decor.
✉ **Glorieta de Bilbao 7** ☎ **91 521 56 55** Ⓜ **Bilbao** ⏰ **Mon-Thur & Sun 8am-1am, Fri & Sat 8am-2am**

Isla de Tesoro
(4, K4) **$$**
Vegetarian
This delightful little joint serves heavenly vegetarian food with a great deal of flair, fun and frivolity. The staff are cheery and the crowds are far from pious, plus the 'treasure island' feel of the decor will make you smile. We also dig the big purple-velvet double bass that you'll see just hanging around.
✉ **Calle de Manuela Malasaña 3** ☎ **91 593 14 40** Ⓜ **San Bernardo or Bilbao** ⏰ **1-4pm & 9-11.30pm** **V**

La Musa (4, K3) **$**
Market
A buzzing disco vibe fills this place even at lunch. Lunch also sees a handy *menú del día* that keeps the Malasaña locals full, satisfied and return customers. We had a great beetroot soup that was full of flavour yet light and refreshing. Nights can get overly crowded, but there's always a nearby plaza for recuperation and some fresh air.
✉ **Calle de Manuela Malasaña 18** ☎ **91 448 75 58** Ⓜ **Bilbao** ⏰ **9am-midnight**

Take some company to Casa do Compañeiro

Eating with Children

Kids are welcome at the vast majority of restaurants, although it's rare to find special menus, portions and high chairs, and the amount of cigarette smoke can irritate young eyes. Look for the ♣ with individual reviews for more child-friendly options.

Nudel Bar (3, C7)   **$$**
Asian
A new addition to Madrid's Asian eateries, and pretty trendy to boot. Things were still getting ironed out when we visited, but the noodle dishes (from Thailand, Vietnam and India) rise above the self-satisfied air that sometimes fills the place.
✉ **Calle de San Bernardino 1** ☎ **91 548 36 40** Ⓜ Noviciado or

Plaza de España
⏰ noon-1am ♣

Siam (3, C7)   **$$$$**
Thai
Beautiful decor touches like stone buddha statues and hanging silks will put you in a mellow state of mind while dining here. The food is the genuine Thai article too, with ingredients flown in especially, and Thai chefs in the kitchen.
✉ **Calle de San Bernardino 6** ☎ **91 559 83 15** Ⓜ Noviciado or Plaza de España
⏰ 1-5pm & 8pm-1am

Tété (3, C8)   **$$$$**
Market
Saved by a whisker or two from being chilly in atmosphere. The seasonal ingredients that feature on the menu are used very imaginatively indeed – we certainly wouldn't have created *sopa de piña con espuma de queso y coco*

(pineapple soup with cheese and coconut foam) in our own kitchen, but it works here.
✉ **Calle Andrés Borrego 16** ☎ **91 522 73 91** Ⓜ Noviciado
⏰ Mon-Fri 2-4pm & 9pm-midnight, Sat 9pm-midnight

Toma (3, B6)   **$$$**
Creative
A rush of red (paint) to the head is what you experience when you walk into this very modern, yet comfy bistro. The chef, Paul Regan, uses his imagination but never brings out the emperor's new clothes. Speaking of which, you may want to don something a little more special to come to this place, even if you're just having a cocktail.
✉ **Calle de Conde Duque 14** ☎ **91 547 49 96** Ⓜ Noviciado
⏰ Tues-Sat 9pm-1am

SALAMANCA & RETIRO

Café-Restaurante El Espejo (3, C15)   **$$**
Café/Basque/French
This café is an attractive and elegant spot to while away the hours. Despite its turn-of-the-century style, it only opened in 1990. The *pabellón* (pavillion) is one of *the* places to have a tipple in summer, and it's all to a pianist's tinkling accompaniment. The more upmarket restaurant ($$$$) serves good Basque/French cuisine. Dress up and make a night of it.
✉ **Paseo de los Recoletos 31** ☎ **91 308 23 47** Ⓜ Colón
⏰ 10.30am-1am

Gran Café de Gijón (3, D14)   **$$**
Café/International
This long-time haunt of literary Madrid has been dishing up coffee, good meals and blood-red velvet decor since 1888. In the winter months, the atmosphere is cosy – in summer you should head outside to the swanky terrace area, where a grand piano sits ready to serenade you, and *cava* (champagne) lightly bubbles away ready to quench your thirst.
✉ **Paseo de los Recoletos 21** ☎ **91 521 54 25** Ⓜ Banco de España ⏰ 7am-2am

Le Divellec (4, J9)   **$$$$**
French
Named after French chef Jacques Le Divellec, this is an excellent choice for those wanting some dining pleasure while they get down to business. Fishy business even, as the food is billed as 'Cuisine de la Mar'. When we visited, chef David Millet was behind the stove, but there were no complaints.
✉ **Hotel Villa Magna, Paseo de la Castellana 22** ☎ **91 587 12 34** Ⓜ Rubén Darío
⏰ Mon-Sat 1-4pm & 8.30-11.30pm

Mumbai Massala
(3, D15) $$$
Indian
A strong contender for the title of Madrid's prettiest restaurant, the stunning pink, gold and glittery decor *almost* competes with the northeast Indian cuisine. Dishes are packed with flavour and service is a joy. Book for weekends, as opening hours are relatively short.
✉ Calle de Recoletos 14 ☎ 91 435 71 94
Ⓜ Banco de España
🚇 Recoletos ⏱ Sun-Thur 1.30-3.30pm & 9-11pm, Fri 1.30-3.30pm & 9pm-midnight, Sat 1.30-4pm & 9pm-midnight **V**

Wine
The standard accompaniment to any meal in Spain, wine comes in three varieties: *tinto* (red), *blanco* (white) and *rosado* (rosé). It can be ordered by the glass (*copa*) or in measures of 500mL or 1L. *Vino de mesa* (table wine) is perfectly decent in most places, but the area around Madrid is not widely regarded as one of Spain's premier wine-producing regions.

Restaurante Oter Epicure (4, K9) $$$$
Navarran
The food here is upmarket Navarran, with a bit of Basque thrown in to ensure everyone's satisfied. The service is smooth. The presentation reveals much effort, and the wine list is a thing of beauty. You might

With a View to...
Our favourite view in Madrid is from the top-floor terrace of **El Viajero** (p91), with its heart-stirring vista of the historic centre's skyline, although the restaurant is on the ground floor. For views over the Casa de Campo, head to **El Molino de los Porches** (p74), with a lovely terrace. **Café-Restaurante El Espejo** (p85) has a swanky terrace perfect for beautiful people watching, but our advice is to find a plaza you like, plonk yourself on a seat and watch the world go by, which can be as intoxicating as any tourist-geared view.

want to dress up and make a reservation.
✉ Calle de Claudio Coello 73 ☎ 91 431 67 71 Ⓜ Velázquez
⏱ Mon-Sat 1-4.30pm & 8.30pm-midnight

Sushi Itto (3, D15) $$
Japanese
As neat and shiny as a new pin, but also casual enough to lose the 'Japanese shrine' atmosphere that can hamper the fun in many such restaurants, this place does great sushi, which can be shared or hogged according to your mood, or even delivered to your hotel.
✉ Calle de Recoletos 10 ☎ 91 426 21 69
Ⓜ Banco de España
🚇 Recoletos ⏱ Sun-Thurs 1.30-4.30pm & 8.30pm-midnight, Fri & Sat 1.30-4.30pm & 8.30pm-1am ♨

Taberna de Daniela (2, K8) $
Tapas
It's easy to overlook the Goya area if tapas and tipples are on your mind, but at midday, this well-tiled, colourful joint attracts quite a few people, and they all seem to be enjoying what's on offer, despite

the fact that service is patchy at times.
✉ Calle del General Pardiñas 21 ☎ 91 575 23 29 Ⓜ Goya
⏱ 11.30am-5.30pm, Sun-Thur 7.30-11.30pm, Fri & Sat 7.30pm-1am

Teatriz (2, K7) $$$$
Italian
Even the toilets are a theatrical experience here – visitors leave luminous footprints on the floor. You'll be spending more than a penny though at this Philippe Starck-designed restaurant, as this is one of Madrid's grooviest. You'll certainly want to put on your glad rags, and reservations are definitely recommended.
✉ Calle de la Hermosilla 15 ☎ 91 577 53 79 Ⓜ Serrano
⏱ 1.30-4pm 9pm-1am ♿

Thai Gardens (2, L6) $$$$
Thai
This is one of those places where the name says it all really. The better than average food is graciously presented, and set in a lavish garden-atmosphere. Ingredients are fresh (they're flown in on a weekly basis from Thailand)

and skilfully handled, plus there's parking. You'd be well advised to make a reservation, especially at weekends.

✉ **Calle de Jorge Juan 5** ☎ 91 577 88 84 Ⓜ Serrano ◷ 2–5pm, Sun–Thur 9pm-1am, Fri & Sat 9pm-2am **V**

Zalacaín (4, F8) $$$$
Creative
The proud possessor of three Michelin stars, Zalacaín is one of Madrid's finest restaurants. It was established by the Oyarbide family in the 1970s, and standards have not slipped, so loosen the belt, unhinge

the wallet and get busy with the menu (after having reserved a table and put on your best duds).
✉ **Calle Álvarez de Baena 4** ☎ 91 561 59 35 Ⓜ Gregorio Marañón ◷ Mon–Fri 1.15-4pm, Mon–Sat 9pm-midnight

SOL & GRAN VÍA

Artemisa (3, E10) $$
Vegetarian
This central vegetarian restaurant is good for animal lovers, with a good varied menu that features tasty salads. The *platos al horno* (oven-baked dishes) are recommended.
✉ **Calle de las Tres Cruces 4** ☎ 91 521 87 21 Ⓜ Gran Vía ◷ 1.30-4pm & 9pm-midnight ⚓ **V**

Casa Labra (3, F10) $
Tapas
Since 1860, madrileños have been squeezing past each other in Casa Labra to get a beer in one hand and some *bacalao croquetas* in the other. Who knows if these *croquetas* were the inspiration for Pablo Iglesias and his comrades to found the Spanish socialist party here over 120 years ago.
✉ **Calle de Tetuán 11** ☎ 91 531 00 81 Ⓜ Sol ◷ Mon–Sat 9.30am-3.30pm & 6-11pm, Sun 1-4pm & 8-11pm

Casa Parrondo (3, E8) $$$
Asturian
Asturian cuisine is staple here, which means lots of chorizo and cheese for tapas and some excellent

main courses, with meat lovers relishing the *cabrales* (rare steak). The restaurant resembles an Asturian house in the mountains and, if the photos of the owner killing pigs doesn't turn your stomach, you'll be rewarded.
✉ **Calle de Trujillos 9** ☎ 91 522 62 34 Ⓜ Santo Domingo ◷ Mon–Sat 1-4pm & 8.30pm-2am, Sun 1-4pm

Delfos (3, E7) $$
Greek
If the name and the decor didn't clue you in that this is a Greek joint, then the food certainly will. The *moysaka* (mousaka) is damn fine, and suits the casual, friendly feel of the place.
✉ **Cuesta de Santo Domingo 14** ☎ 91 548 37 64 Ⓜ Santo Domingo ◷ Tues–Sun 12.30-4pm & 8.30pm-midnight

Gula Gula (3, E12) $$$
Theatre restaurant
Gula Gula's salad buffet is a veritable sea of greenery in an otherwise meat-loving Madrid. The other reason for coming here though is so you can feast on the nightly drag-queen shows, which are spicy, but not so

risqué as to shock the mainstream.
✉ **Gran Vía 1** ☎ 91 522 87 64 Ⓜ Banco de España ◷ Tues–Sun 1-4.30pm, Tues–Thur & Sun 9pm-1.30am, Fri & Sat 9pm-2.30am **V**

Dinner Deals
If you're in Madrid for business, good places to make an impression include: **Santceloni** (p75), **Zalacaín** (p87), **Le Divellec** (p85), **Santo Mauro** (p76), **El Bodegon** (p75), **East 47** (p79) as well as **Restaurante Oter Epicure** (p86).

Restaurante La Paella Real (3, F7) $$$
Paella/Valencian
Paella does not originate from Madrid, but many visitors believe that to eat Spanish is to eat paella. Luckily, you can find it here, and no matter where it's from, it's good stuff. This place offers more than paella though, with a large selection for rice lovers.
✉ **Calle de Arrieta 2** ☎ 91 542 09 42 Ⓜ Ópera ◷ 1-4pm ⚓

entertainment

The reason it's a cliché is because it's true – *madrileños* really don't end the night until they've killed it. It's the perfect place for making merry, with a plethora of bars (over 20,000!), great gay nightlife, all-night-long dance clubs, and a whirl of flamenco, jazz, salsa and rock venues. If the more old-fashioned arts are your cup of tea, the theatre scene is lively, the opera is sterling, classical music is appreciated and modern dance, well, it's getting there. Locals love nothing more than going to the movies on a Sunday. All this plus local festivals and city-sponsored events means you can be busy indeed.

Locals *are* as passionate about social life as you've heard, and the hours they keep are startling. Don't even think about starting a big night before midnight. Dancing won't begin until around 3am. Bed time? About 6am – well, maybe.

Top Spots

Madrid's top nightlife area surrounds the Plaza de Santa Ana, with literally hundreds of bars and thousands of people, from the young and not-so-young to the avowedly local and a variety of nationalities. Other popular areas include Malasaña, which attracts a grungy, youthful crowd, and Lavapiés, with a good mix of traditional and quirky nightspots. The upwardly mobile set generally frequents the Salamanca *barrio*, while lovers of gay nightlife flock to Chueca.

Tickets & Listings

The weekly *Guía del Ocio* is a must for keeping abreast of what's on. *In Madrid*, a free English-language rag, is also a good source of information, while tourist offices can help with tracking down events and will have information on the arts scene. You can also try *El País* and *El Mundo*, which publish entertainment listings, or the free *El Duende de Madrid*.

Tickets for plays, concerts and other performances can be bought at the theatre concerned, and a few lottery-ticket booths sell theatre, football and bullfight tickets. Madrid Rock (3, E10; ☎ 91 521 02 39) and FNAC (3, E9; ☎ 91 520 00 00) sell tickets to major concerts.

Telephone and Internet bookings are also possible. Try the Caixa de Catalunya (☎ 902 10 12 12, **e** www.caixacatalunya.es), with tickets to many major events and concerts, and Caja de Madrid (☎ 902 48 84 88), which also sells cinema tickets. Like all credit-card bookings, you pay by card and then collect the tickets from the relevant venue.

SPECIAL EVENTS

January *New Year's Eve* – people eat a grape for each chime, for good luck
Día de los Reyes Magos – 6 Jan; a parade of the three kings winds its way around the city to the delight of kids

February/March *Carnevales* – days of fancy-dress parades and merrymaking across the Comunidad de Madrid, usually ending on the Tuesday 47 days before Easter Sunday

May *Fiesta de la Comunidad de Madrid* – 2 May; celebrations are kicked off with a speech by a local personality from the balcony of the Casa de Correos in the Puerta del Sol, and a host of cultural events and festivities follow
Fiestas de San Isidro – 15 May; the big one! Feast day of the city's patron saint followed by a week of partying. The country's most prestigious *feria*, or bullfighting season, also begins now and continues for a month, at the Plaza de Toros Monumental de Las Ventas

June/July *Local Fiestas* – most districts in Madrid celebrate the feast day of one saint or another; ask the tourist office for details of where and when these local knees-ups take place

July–August *Veranos de la Villa* – council-organised arts festival with something for everyone, day and night, whether it be film, dance, music, theatre, photography, art or fashion
Fiestas de San Lorenzo, San Cayetano & La Virgen de la Paloma – 27 Jul-15 Aug; these three local patron saints' festivities (which revolve around La Latina, Plaza de Lavapiés and Calle de Calatrava in La Latina, respectively) keep the central districts of Madrid busy for the best part of three weeks

September *Local Fiestas* – local councils organise fiestas in the first and second weeks of September; these are very local affairs and provide a rare insight into *barrio* life of the average madrileño
Fiesta del PCE – mid-Sept; the Spanish Communist Party holds its annual fundraiser in the Casa de Campo, a weekend-long mixed bag of regional-food pavilions, rock concerts and political soap-boxing

November *Día de la Virgen de la Almudena* – 9 Nov; *castizos* (true-blue madrileños) gather in Plaza Mayor to hear Mass on this the feast day of the city's female patron saint

BARS

Bar Cock (3, E11)
Once a salon for high-class prostitution, Bar Cock retains a gentlemen's club atmosphere, although the crowd is often comprised of resolutely with-it 30-somethings in linen, leather, lace and polo-neck sweaters. You have to knock to get in, and apparently a table stands reserved for the prince.
✉ **Calle de la Reina 16**
☎ **91 532 28 26**
Ⓜ **Gran Vía** ☺ **Mon-Sat 9pm-4am**

Sexy Bodega Melibea

Bodega Melibea
(3, G10) Owned by the same sexy crowd as the Matador Bar (see p91–2), this is *the* place to come if cheap red wine and Sapphic-themed tiles are your thing, you like to watch, or you just appreciate a chatty atmosphere.
✉ **Calle de Espoz y Mina 9** Ⓜ **Sol**
☺ **7pm-2am**

Café Belén (3, C12)
If the streets surrounding this bar are getting a little *too* young for you, then relax. You and your grown-up friends can sit and listen to an eclectic selection of music without shouting at each other, all while enjoying excellent cocktails (especially the *mojitos*).
✉ **Calle de Belén 5**
☎ **91 308 27 47**
Ⓜ **Chueca or Alonso Martínez**
☺ **3.30pm-3am**

Casa Pueblo (3, H12)
The Casa Pueblo is a cosy place where the young-at-heart (but no longer very young) can enjoy a cocktail and listen to jazz, still played on an old reel-to-reel. It's warm, welcoming, and a nice alternative to the Santa Ana scene.
✉ **Calle de León 3**
☎ **91 429 05 15**
Ⓜ **Antón Martín**
☺ **Tues-Sat 10pm-2.30am, Sun 10pm-3.30am**

Del Diego (3, E11)
For a bar with a blonde-wood Art Deco look going on and waiters who appear to have been inspired by the Chris Isaak school of grooming, Del Diego has a surprisingly casual (dare we say ordinary?) crowd piling in for some very smooth cocktails.
✉ **Calle de la Reina 12**
☎ **91 523 31 06**
Ⓜ **Gran Vía** ☺ **Mon-Sat 9pm-3am**

El Café de Shéhérazad (3, J12)
Quite a romantic spot, given the authentic Islamic kit-out (right down to the beautiful stonework and smoking equipment). You can drink mint tea and all manner of alcoholic drinks, and the attentive and charming staff will make you swoon.
✉ **Calle de Santa María 18** ☎ **91 369 24 74** Ⓜ **Antón Martín**
☺ **7pm-3am**

El Eucalipto (2, O4)
El Eucalipto makes some of the best *mojitos* we've ever had, which is saying something in this cocktail-loving town. The vibe is friendly and chatty, partly because this particular street has a reputation for a breezy, unpretentious atmosphere, especially when there's outdoor seating in summer.
✉ **Calle de Argumosa 4** Ⓜ **Lavapiés**
☺ **6pm-2am**

No Smoke Without Fire

Drug laws in Spain were tightened in 1992, and while marijuana (often called *maría*) is legal for personal use, public consumption is not. You may well find people smoking a joint (*porro*) in bars or in plazas, but you might want to think twice before you join in, as most cops won't have a problem with arresting a foolish foreigner. For the record, hash is also known as 'chocolate', which can lead to a little confusion for some.

El 21 (3, H8)
A shoebox of a place that hasn't seen a lick of paint in years, everything here seems stained a rich shade of nicotine. It's charmingly scruffy, with courteous regulars (young and old) and blindingly cheap drinks. We're tempted to make it one of our 'Highlights', but you wouldn't all fit.
✉ **Calle de Toledo 21** ☎ **91 366 28 59** Ⓜ **La Latina** ☺ **Mon-Thur & Sun noon-3.30pm & 7-11pm, Fri & Sat noon-3.30pm & 7pm-midnight**

El Viajero (3, J6)
The ground floor serves great organic steaks, but we prefer to venture upstairs, where the first floor offers a bar with great music (dub, acid jazz and funk) and the second floor has our favourite terrace in Madrid, with views of the area's skyline. Get in early or book ahead.
✉ **Plaza de la Cebada 11** ☎ **91 366 90 64** Ⓜ **La Latina** ☺ **Tues-Sat 2pm-2.30am, Sun 1pm-8pm**

La Divina Comedia (3, K13) A young, attractive crowd drops in here to get its fill of *mojitos* and enjoy a neo-bordello, Frida Kahlo-tribute atmosphere. It's all red walls, a fair few cushions, some tea candles and DJ-spun sounds, which include acid jazz, cruisy house and a bit of reggae.
✉ **Calle de Almadén 14** Ⓜ **Anton Martín** ☺ **Tues-Sun 7pm-2am**

La Falsa Molestia (3, J11) Something of a pale-coloured beauty spot for those hanging around this side of town. It's supposed to be Italian-style, and while there are good Italian wines on offer, we're struggling to remember too many bars in Italy that were this attractive.
✉ **Calle de Magdalena 32** ☎ **91 420 32 38** ⓔ **www.lafalsamolestia.com** Ⓜ **Antón Martín** ☺ **Wed-Sun 1pm-3am**

Los Gabrieles (3, G11) Bringing new meaning to the phrase 'a night on the tiles', this popular bar has some of the most impressive tilework in Madrid (check out the skeleton playing guitar). It used to be a brothel and there's free flamenco Tuesday to Thursday in July. What more could you want?
✉ **Calle de Echegaray 17** ☎ **91 429 62 61** Ⓜ **Sevilla** ☺ **Mon-Thur & Sun 1pm-2am, Fri & Sat 1pm-3am**

Maderfaker (3, B10) Someone here has seen *Shaft* and really loved it, hence the name of this place (say it with a Spanish accent!). We really love it because it's a lively spot, without being too crowded or brash, and is therefore the perfect spot to psyche yourself up for later on.
✉ **Calle de San Vicente Ferrer 17** Ⓜ **Tribunal** ☺ **Tues-Sat 11pm-3.30am**

Magic Room (3, C10) The night-loving hordes of this night-loving district flock here on a regular basis to soak up the spacey-meets-psychedelic ambience and a good amount of booze. The crowd has an anything-goes quality that makes the name pertinent, and the music choices include Latin-house, 70's disco and house on weekends.
✉ **Calle de Colón 12** ☎ **91 531 34 91** Ⓜ **Tribunal or Chueca** ☺ **Tues-Sun 11.30pm-5am**

Matador Bar (3, G10) Playing good flamenco music, this popular bar has been going since 1994. The bar staff are on the dishy side, which is a good thing for the young types frequenting this place, although God knows who got the idea that extremely detailed, amateurish drawings of genitalia were good

Heady Stuff

If you've arrived from England, Australia, or any country where the head on your beer must be 'just so', Madrid will surprise you. Heads on beer can seem to take up half the glass, especially if you're drinking a *caña* (small glass). While some bartenders will wield a spatula-like utensil to shave off excess, the initial problem seems to stem from a refusal to tilt the glass when pouring. You may also wonder why beers are slammed down in front of you, as though you've incurred the bartender's wrath. Relax, it's to settle the head.

decor practice. Thankfully the staff are good looking.
✉ **Calle de la Cruz 39**
☎ **91 531 89 91**
Ⓜ **Sol** ☺ **Tues-Sun 7pm-2am**

Mi Gente (3, K10)
Got a grandparent whose garage is chock-full of old furniture, useless knick-knacks and a few items that are unclassifiables? Now add a small bar. A no-frills, no-fuss establishment with an endearingly laid-back, rough-round-the-edges clientele with special appearances by Lucas the dog. The music's cool too –

think flamenco, blues, and, er, The Police.
✉ **Calle de Olmo 3**
Ⓜ **Antón Martín**
☺ **midnight-erratic**

Museo Chicote (3, E11) A sense of tradition hangs over this Art Deco bar, which is a remnant from the 1940s and 50s when this was considered Madrid's swankiest watering hole, with the likes of Ernest Hemingway and Ava Gardner stopping by. Service is old-school, and so are the cocktails.
✉ **Gran Vía 12** ☎ **91 532 67 37** Ⓜ **Gran Vía**

☺ **Mon-Thur 9am-3am, Fri & Sat 9am-4am**

Viva Madrid (3, G11)
A damn fine spot for some early-evening tippling. It's fine too in the late evening, if you enjoy fighting your way through the heaving crowds (locals and tourists), all wanting liquid refreshment. Keep a lookout for the tiles, they're worth the trip alone.
✉ **Calle de Manuel Fernández y González 7**
☎ **91 429 36 40**
Ⓜ **Sevilla** ☺ **Sun-Thur 1pm-2am, Fri & Sat 1pm-3am**

DANCE CLUBS & DISCOS

Fortuny (4, H8)
If you fancy a nightclub with a little more style than most, Fortuny comes heartily recommended by the *pijos* (yuppies). It's in a renovated palace, but the sometimes-ferocious door policy will keep you out if you chose your shoes mostly for comfort. The music's unadventurous.
✉ **Calle de Fortuny 34**
☎ **91 319 05 88**
Ⓜ **Rubén Darío**
☺ **midnight-5am**
⑤ **€8**

Joy Eslava (3, F8)
Going strong for 20 years in a building that dates back to 1872, it's something of an institution, and you never know what mix the club's going to attract on any given night. High types, low types, gays, straights, young and old – they all like gilt-tinged decor and a guilt-free boogy. Head to Chocolatería de San Ginés

(see p46) after if you're still going around breakfast.
✉ **Calle del Arenal 11**
☎ **91 366 37 33**
ⓔ **www.joy-eslava.com**
Ⓜ **Sol** ☺ **Sun-Thur 11.30pm-5.30am, Fri & Sat 11.30pm-6am**
⑤ **€12-15**

Kapital (2, O6)
There are seven, yes, seven floors (but no elevator!) of nocturnal entertainment here, ranging from dance music, karaoke, galleries and a cinema, with a writhing, sexily clad crowd lapping it all up. Kapital also runs 'afternoon' sessions for the young folk.
✉ **Calle de Atocha 125**
☎ **91 420 29 06**
Ⓜ **Atocha** ☺ **early sessions Sat, Sun & hols 5.30-11pm, late sessions Thurs-Sun midnight-6am** ⑤ **€6**

Morocco (3, D8)
Still a popular stop on the night-owl circuit, although

it's getting a little more sophisticated with time. The music is varied and can include anything from disco lip-synch faves to the more experimental.
✉ **Calle del Marqués de Leganés 7** ☎ **91 531 31 77** Ⓜ **Santo Domingo** ☺ **Thur midnight-3am, Fri & Sat 9pm-5.30am** ⑤ **free**

Ohm (3, E9)
A popular night at the Bash Line club for those in the mood to 'wave your hands in the air like you just don't care'. We saw all types letting it all hang out. This is a must for those who like crowds and inclusive DJs.
✉ **Plaza del Callao 4**
☎ **91 531 01 32**
Ⓜ **Callao** ☺ **Fri & Sat midnight-6am** ⑤ **€10**

Palacio Gaviria (3, F8)
This place really used to be a palace and the luxury trimmings are still evident.

People get pretty dressed up, and the queues can be disheartening. Despite its exclusive overtones, it's not frighteningly posh, with Salsa (Tues), Cabaret (Wed), 'Exchange' (Thur – lots of international snogging) and lots of disco on the weekend. Much fun.
✉ **Calle del Arenal 9**
☎ **91 526 60 69**
e **www.palaciogaviria .com** Ⓜ **Sol** ◷ **Tues & Wed 10.30pm-3.30am, Thur-Sat 11pm-6am, Sun 10.30pm-3am** Ⓢ **€12**

Space of Sound
(2, A7) If you're still going from the night before, then you'll meet plenty of like-minded souls at Space of Sound, where too much house and techno are never enough. And hey, at least you know the metro's started up again, so you can get home easily when you're finally ready to collapse.
✉ **Plaza de Estación de Chamartín**

Disco Discounts
Many of Madrid's streets are littered with brightly coloured cards and flyers in the morning, but it can be a good idea to accept these proffered papers and have a closer look – many offer reduced entry to bars and clubs, and not just the ones that you think must be desperate for business. Conditions often apply (such as entry before 3am), but please, if you're going to discard a card, use the bin!

☎ **91 733 35 05**
Ⓜ **Chamartín** ◷ **Sun 9am-7pm** Ⓢ **€6**

Suite (3, F11)
There's a restaurant/café here, and it's not a bad 'quiet drink' spot (especially if you happen to be a devotee of *wallpaper** magazine), but we like it when things kick-off after midnight on weekends – that's when everyone's shaking out the cobwebs on the suspended dance floor to some seriously funky DJ sounds.
✉ **Calle Virgen de los Peligros 4** ☎ **91 521**

---

40 31 Ⓜ **Sevilla** ◷ **Mon-Sat 11.30am-3.30am** Ⓢ **free**

The Room (3, G11)
The Room is absolutely packed by about 3am, so you'll need to arrive well before then to ensure that you get the chance to dance to one of Madrid's best DJs, Ángel García. A vibrant, heady place, with some great visuals, even if you're almost cross-eyed from partying.
✉ **Calle de Arlabán 7**
☎ **91 523 86 54**
Ⓜ **Sevilla** ◷ **Fri & Sat 1am-6am** Ⓢ **€8**

CINEMAS

Standard cinema tickets cost around €5.50, but many cinemas have at least one day set aside as the *día del espectador* (viewer's day) with cut-price tickets (usually about €2 off). You can purchase tickets at the cinemas or in advance (in some cases) on ☎ 902 48 84 88 or online at e www.guiade locio.com.

Alphaville (3, C5)
This is the place to come to avoid mainstream foreign fare and mix it with a few arty types, as it shows original-language films with a more independent streak than other cinemas in Madrid. There are four screens, and three theatres have wheelchair access.
✉ **Calle de Martín de los Heros 14** ☎ **91 559**

Cine Doré

38 36 Ⓜ **Plaza de España** ◷ **daily from 4.30pm** Ⓢ **€5.50 (Mon €3.50)**

Cine Doré (3, J11)
The Cine Doré is a delightful old cinema, housing the Filmoteca Nacional (national film library), and you can expect to see classics old and new, in their original languages. There's also a

library and bar/restaurant attached (open 4pm-midnight).

✉ Calle de Santa Isabel 3 ☎ 91 549 00 11 Ⓜ Antón Martín ⏱ three sessions from 6pm Ⓢ (1.35, abono (10-ticket pass) €10.20

Imax Madrid (1, E3)
Well, we don't know what the 3D fuss is about, but kids dig it. It's also housed in the same park as the Planetario de Madrid. Prebook at Caixa Catalunya (☎ 902 10 12 12), El Corte Inglés (☎ 902 400 222) or ⓔ www.telentrada.com (see p62).
✉ Parque Enrico Tierno Galván, Legazpi

☎ 91 467 48 00 Ⓜ Méndez Álvaro ⏱ Mon-Fri 1pm-10pm; Sat, Sun & hols noon-11pm Ⓢ one/two sessions €6.60/9.60 (Mon €5.40) ♿

Princesa (3, B6)
This cinema – like its neighbour – is owned by the Renoir group, but it is bigger, with nine theatres (one with wheelchair access) and has a much better selection of films. There are also prebooking possibilities which are the same for Renoir Plaza de España (see following).
✉ Calle de Princesa 3 ☎ 91 541 41 00 Ⓜ Plaza de España ⏱ daily from 4pm

Ⓢ adult/concession €5.40/4 ♿

Renoir Plaza de España (3, C5)
This is part of a chain of cinemas that all specialise in original-language films (there is another at Calle de Princesa 5). The theatres all have excellent facilities and you can pre-book your tickets on the Web at ⓔ www.guiadelocio.com and by telephone on ☎ 902 888 902.
✉ Calle de Martín de los Heros 12 ☎ 91 541 41 00 Ⓜ Plaza de España ⏱ daily from 4.15pm (plus 12.30pm Fri & Sat) Ⓢ adult/concession €5.40/4 ♿

LIVE MUSIC VENUES

Café Central (3, H10)
This is probably Madrid's best place to hear live jazz, with both local and international acts deigning to play here. The atmosphere's good too – you're close to the stage without feeling as though you're in a broom closet, and there's an intimate, low-key vibe.
✉ Plaza de Ángel 10 ☎ 91 369 41 43 Ⓜ Sol or Antón Martín ⏱ Mon-Thur 1pm-2.30am, Fri & Sat 1pm-3.30am Ⓢ about €10

Café Populart
(3, H11) A small and intimate, yet lively venue with a tiny stage and some pretty smart service. You can enjoy blues, jazz, Cuban, reggae, flamenco and swing here.
✉ Calle de las Huertas 22 ☎ 91 429 84 07 ⓔ www.populart.es

Ⓜ Antón Martín ⏱ shows at 11pm & 12.30pm

Clamores (4, J5)
Away from the throbbing centre of Madrid's nightlife, Clamores gets a well-regarded selection of jazz artists to play here. Another bonus is the

Off-beat Café Central

greater freedom of movement that comes with the non-*centro* premises.
✉ Calle de Alburquerque 14 ☎ 91 445 79 38 Ⓜ Bilbao ⏱ Mon-Thur & Sun 6pm-3am, Fri & Sat 6pm-4am, shows at 10pm Ⓢ €3-6

El Sol (3, E11)
Independent bands (local and foreign) get a live airing here before the funk takes over, and it's a bit of a haven for those who want a slightly grungier, crimson-lit atmosphere. Not as important as it was in the 1980s *movida* scene, but still very lively.
✉ Calle de los Jardines 3 ☎ 91 532 64 90 Ⓜ Gran Via ⏱ Concerts from 11.30pm, otherwise Tues-Sat 12.30pm-5am Ⓢ €8

Galileo Galilei (4, F2)
Enthusiasts of live Latin music will enjoy a visit here. The music dominates your attention, but there are also photographic exhibitions at times. It's a good space too, with room to breathe and to move (should the mood take you).
✉ **Calle de Galileo 100**
☎ **91 534 75 57**
🅴 **www.salagalileo galilei.com** Ⓜ **Canal**
🕐 6pm-4.30am
⑤ €5-10

Moby Dick (2, E6)
In the northern part of town and featuring regular shows by local bands, this is a good spot to catch up on your Spanish rock and pop. DJs keep the crowd buzzing after the show's over.
✉ **Avenida del Brasil 5**
☎ **91 555 76 71**

Ⓜ **Santiago Bernabéu**
🕐 Mon-Sat 10pm-3am
⑤ free

Suristán (3, G11)
Suristán prides itself on offering a variety of live music acts, and the pride is justified. It's a chilled-out, yet lively place to enjoy a plethora of music styles, including African, Cuban, Celtic and Spanish, and the need to dance hits your feet fast.
✉ **Calle de la Cruz 7**
☎ **91 532 39 09**
🅴 **www.suristan.com**
Ⓜ **Sevilla** 🕐 10pm-5am ⑤ €7

Popular artists at Populart, p94

FLAMENCO

Café de Chinitas
(3, E6) A cut above many flamenco joints, but you'll need to book to dine and enjoy the shows here. Famous past audience members include Bill Clinton and the King of Spain, and the performers are often well known too.
✉ **Calle de Torija 7**
☎ **91 559 51 35**
🅴 **www.chinitas.com**
Ⓜ **Santo Domingo**
🕐 Mon-Sat 9pm-2.30am, show at 10.30pm ⑤ dinner & show from €66 ♿

Cardamomo (3, G11)
Many locals with a love of flamenco were thrilled when this place opened recently. Performances take place Wed 10.30pm, and there's always good music

on offer even if you miss one of these. It's a dark, stylish and sexy place – the perfect background for the good-looking patrons, staff and performers.
✉ **Calle Echegaray 15**
☎ **91 369 07 57**
Ⓜ **Sevilla** 🕐 9pm-4am
⑤ free

Casa Patas (3, J10)
This is an excellent and comfortable space to enjoy recognised masters of flamenco guitar, song and dance. Famous faces can often be found both on stage and in the crowd, and you'd do well to book in advance. Courses in flamenco can also be organised and good food is available.
✉ **Calle de Cañizares 10** ☎ **91 369 04 96**

🅴 **www.casapatas.com**
Ⓜ **Antón Martín**
🕐 Mon-Sat noon-5pm & 8pm-12.30am, shows at 10.30pm Mon-Fri, at 9pm & midnight Sat & Sun ⑤ about €15

Corral de la Morería
(3, J5) This is another dinner-and-a-show tablao (tourist-oriented flamenco), but this one is actually worth considering. It's not as big and flash as some of the others, but the quality's good so you won't feel as though you've just wandered into and been caught in a tourist trap.
✉ **Calle de la Morería 17** ☎ **91 365 84 46**
Ⓜ **La Latina** 🕐 9pm-2am, show at 10.45pm
⑤ from €25

Las Carboneras
(3, H7) This place is something of a young gun, or rather a young guitar, on the flamenco scene, and has a cosy feel. The stage lies to your right as you enter and you can set your sights on the bar, which is dead ahead. Performers are not from the heady, older strato-sphere, but they're pretty good, and always brim-ming with spunky young energy.
✉ Plaza del Conde de Miranda 1 ☎ 91 542 86 77 Ⓜ Sol
🕐 8.30pm-2am, show at 10.30pm Ⓢ free

Duende
Duende is the heart and soul of flamenco, but trying to come up with a definitive description of it is no mean feat. It's that moment when a performer seems to disappear into their art. It's what poet García Lorca described as 'black sounds'. The best way we can think of recognising it is when the hairs on the back of your neck stand up, your eyes are pricked with tears, a shiver goes down your spine and the locals are all calling out 'Olé!'.

CLASSICAL MUSIC, OPERA, DANCE & THEATRE

Auditorio Nacional de Música (2, G8)
Don't let the hideously ugly exterior put you off too much. The inside is more than comfortable and, most importantly if you're listening to music, it's great for acoustics. This auditorium is also the home of La Orquestra y Coro Nacionales de España (Spain's national orchestra), which means you can feast on classical music from October to June.
✉ Calle del Príncipe de Vergara 146
☎ 91 337 01 39
☎ box office 91 337 03 07 or 902 488 488
ℯ www.auditorio nacional.mcu.es
Ⓜ Cruz del Rayo or Prosperidad 🕐 box office Mon 5-7pm, Tues-Fri 10am-5pm, Sat 10am-1pm Ⓢ varies ♿ rehearsal attendance – check with theatre

Centro Cultural Conde Duque (3, A6)
Also known as the Antiguo Cuartel del Conde Duque, this massive structure has some excellent shows, especially during summer and the Veranos de la Villa festival. The variety of acts on offer is mind-boggling.
✉ Calle de Conde Duque 11 ☎ 91 588 58 34 Ⓜ Ventura Rodríguez or Noviciado 🕐 box office 5pm per-formance day; centre Tues-Sat 10am-2pm & 5.30-9pm, Sun 10.30am-2.30pm Ⓢ varies ♿

Centro Cultural de la Villa (3, B15)
If you're having trouble finding this theatre, look under the waterfall at Plaza de Colón. You'll find per-formances of classical music, comic theatre, fla-menco, exhibitions, as well as stuff that'll please the

kids in this 800-plus capacity venue.
✉ Plaza de Colón
☎ 91 575 60 80 or 902 101 212 Ⓜ Colón 🕐 Tues-Sun 11am-1.30pm & 5-6pm Ⓢ varies ♿ kids' theatre performances

Fundación Juan March (4, J11)
This important foundation has been a boost to Madrid's artistic scene since the 1950s, and apart from hosting exhibitions, it's also a good source of musical performances (for young and old).
✉ Calle de Castelló 77
☎ 91 435 42 40
Ⓜ Núñez de Balboa 🕐 Mon-Sat 10am-2pm & 5.30-9pm, Sun 10am-2pm Ⓢ free ♿

Teatro Albéniz
(3, G9) A variety of per-formances are staged here, from opera and *zarzuela*

(Spanish light opera) to plays and dance (including flamenco). If you're here in August, don't miss the chance to see Alicia Alonso's Ballet Nacional de Cuba perform the ballet classics, which happens every year.
✉ **Calle de la Paz 11**
☎ **91 531 83 11 or 902 488 488** Ⓜ **Sol**
🕐 box office 11.30am-1pm & 5.30-9pm
💲 varies

Teatro de la Zarzuela (3, G12)

The Spanish version of light opera is known as *zar-zuela*, and this is the best place to experience it. The theatre, built in 1856 in a vague imitation of Milan's La Scala also stages ballets and music recitals.
✉ **Calle de Jovellanos 4** ☎ **91 524 54 00, box office 902 488 488**
🌐 **http://teatro delazarzuela.mcu.es**
Ⓜ **Banco de España or Sevilla** 🕐 box office daily noon-6pm (to 8pm performance days)
💲 €10-180 ♿ kids' matinees Wed 6pm

Teatro Español

(3, H11) A theatre has stood on this spot since 1583. Known as the Teatro Español since 1849, the repertoire consists mostly of contemporary Spanish drama and some gems from the 17th century. It's

a beautiful theatre, and worth a visit even if you understand nothing of what's being said.
✉ **Calle del Príncipe 25** ☎ **91 429 62 97**
Ⓜ **Sol or Sevilla**
🕐 box office Tues-Sun 11.30am-1.30pm, Tues-Thur & Sun 5-7pm, Fri & Sat 5-6.30pm & 8-9.30pm, shows Tues-Thur & Sun 8pm, Fri & Sat 7.30pm & 10.30pm
💲 €5-16

Teatro Monumental

(3, J12) A decent theatre, though not in the same league as the Teatro Real. One reason to come here is to hear the RTVE Orquestra Sinfónica y Coro. School groups and children are often allowed in to watch rehearsals on Thursday mornings, but you'll need to book for this.
✉ **Calle de Atocha 65**
☎ **91 429 12 81 or**

902 488 488
🌐 **www.rtve.es**
Ⓜ **Antón Martín**
🕐 box office Oct-May daily 11am-2pm & 5-7pm, concerts Oct-May Tues-Thur 8pm
💲 €5.50-14 ♿ re-hearsals Thur morning

Teatro Real (3, F6)

The grandest stage in the city and one of the world's most technically advanced theatres. Acoustics are superb, seats are comfy and at intermission you can en-joy lovely views over Plaza de Oriente and the Palacio Real. Catch opera, ballet, classical music and flamen-co (July) performances here.
✉ **Plaza de Oriente**
☎ **91 516 06 06**
🌐 **www.teatroreal .com** Ⓜ **Ópera**
🕐 box office Mon-Sat 10am-1.30pm & 5.30-8pm 💲 €12-21
♿ matinees

Teatro Español

GAY & LESBIAN MADRID

Cafe Aquarela

(3, C12) The decor here is part colonial gentlemen's club and part opium den. This smallish bar is great to replenish the thirst you've earned after a hard

day; or to start the mood before a big night. The crowd? There are lesbians on first dates, gay men on last dates, as well as everything in between. The bar staff on the night we

went were capable, yet up themselves.
✉ **Calle de Gravina 10**
☎ **91 522 21 43**
Ⓜ **Chueca** 🕐 Mon-Thur 3pm-3am, Fri & Sat 3pm-4am

El Mojito
(3, K11) Perhaps you're growing tired of the Chueca scene? If so, head to this place, where the Ken and Barbie dolls have been arranged in poses so suggestive and sometimes ludicrous it never fails to raise a smile. And the cocktails are good too.
✉ **Calle del Olmo 6**
Ⓜ **Antón Martín**
🕐 Mon-Thur & Sun 10pm-2.30am, Fri & Sat 10pm-3.30am Ⓢ free

Into the Tank
(2, O3) There's a varied, albeit strict, dress code (leather, latex, skinhead and military) and plenty of casual sex on offer, plus a 'basement'. It's strictly for men only.
✉ **Calle de Calatrava 29** 🇪 **www.into thetank.org**

Gay Pride
Madrid's gay and lesbian pride festival and parade take place on the last Saturday in June. It's known as the *Día del Orgullo de Gays, Lesbians y Transexuales* and the partying is intense, intrepid and inspiring.

Aquarela, p97

Ⓜ **La Latina or Puerta de Toledo** 🕐 Thurs & Sun 11pm-5am; Fri, Sat & hols 2am-8am
Ⓢ €10

Mama Inés Café
(3, D11) Come to Mama indeed! Day or night, this is a popular hang-out for the stylish yet casual and mostly gay clientele. During the day, you can treat this place as a café, but things get busier at night, when you can head downstairs and have a dance, or just prop up the well-stocked bar.
✉ **Calle de Hortaleza 22** ☎ **91 523 23 33**
🇪 **www.mamaines.com**
Ⓜ **Gran Via or Chueca**
🕐 Sun-Thur 10am-2am, Fri & Sat 10am-3am Ⓢ free

Medea
(3, J10) Madrid's gay scene is famously open to all, but for those nights when it's the sisterhood or nothing, you can try Medea. The girl-friendly establishment has good music and a pool table, and none of Chueca's madness.
✉ **Calle de la Cabeza 33** Ⓜ **Antón Martín**
🕐 Thur-Sat 11pm-5am Ⓢ free

Rick's
(3, E11) Sooner or later, everyone comes to Rick's. It's not that it's a particularly great place, it's just that it's a bit of an institution that's popular with local and out-of-town gays (mostly men). Look for the purple and black exterior and dive right in, if you can find space.
✉ **Calle de Clavel 8**
Ⓜ **Gran Via**
🕐 11pm-late Ⓢ free

Shangay Tea Dance
(3, D7) Even the toilets are the last word in style here! Cool Ballroom hosts the Shangay Tea Dance every Sunday. An incredibly good-looking crowd is often entertainment in itself, but the DJs deserve a special mention for dishing up house music that gets you right where you live.
✉ **Calle de Isabel la Católica 6** ☎ **91 542 34 39** 🇪 **www.coolball room.com** Ⓜ **Santo Domingo** 🕐 Sun 9pm-2am Ⓢ €6

Star's Dance Café
(3, E12) The gay community appreciates the fact that you can eat, drink and dance here till the wee hours. The straight community likes it too. In fact, everyone likes it here, especially because the decor is attractive, the lighting is flattering and the DJs know how to please.
✉ **Calle del Marqués del Valdeiglesias 5**
☎ **91 522 27 12**
🇪 **www.starscafe dance.com** Ⓜ **Banco de España or Sevilla**
🕐 Mon-Wed 9am-2am, Thur 9am-3am, Fri 9am-4am, Sat 6.30pm-4am Ⓢ free

Strong Center
(3, F8) Time to toughen up and get the leather out! For *hombres* only, this place is not for the faint-hearted or faint-cocked. The dark room (intentionally, so that you use other senses) is famous, or infamous, depending on who you're talking to.
✉ **Calle de Trujillo 7**
☎ **91 531 48 27**
Ⓜ **Callao** 🕐 midnight-6am Ⓢ €6

SPECTATOR SPORTS

See the Tickets & Listings section (p88) for details of buying tickets.

Athletics

Post-Barcelona, athletics has had something of a boost in Spain, and Madrid's bid to host the 2012 Olympics means that facilities are a priority. The **Estadio de la Comunidad de Madrid** (1, E4; ☎ 91 580 51 80; Avenida de Arcentales, Canillejas; Ⓜ Las Musas) is a great high-tech athletics arena, built in 1994 and hosting various events (including the 9th World Cup in Athletics in September 2002). On the last Sunday in April, the Maratón Popular de Madrid is held. You can get information at ⓔ www.maratonmadrid.com.

Basketball

Palacio de los Deportes (2, L9; ☎ 91 401 91 00; Avenida Felipe II, Salamanca; Ⓜ Goya) is the place to see basketball (*baloncesto*). When we visited, it was being rebuilt after a fire, but it should be ready by April 2003, with improved facilities. Madrid's two main basketball teams are Real Madrid (ⓔ www.realmadrid.es) yes, they play basketball too!) and Adecco Estudiantes (ⓔ www.clubestudiantes.com). The season takes place from September to May.

Bullfighting

You've got to admit, any life-and-death sport where the manifestation of prowess and skill involves donning pink silk socks and a skin-tight sequined suit is going to be interesting. Worth seeing is the Feria de San Isidro (Festival of San Isidro), which takes place from mid-May and lasts into June. Tickets for this can be hard to come by though. Regular *corridas* (fights) take place from March to October, generally on Sunday at 7pm. Bullfights take place at the beautiful, enormous **Plaza de Toros**

You big bully

Monumental de Las Ventas (see also p45; 2, J10; ☎ 91 356 22 00; Calle de Alcalá 237; Ⓜ Las Ventas). Tickets cost from €3.50 for a spot in the sun *(sol)* to €105 for a spot in the shade *(sombra)*, and can be purchased at the ticket office at the ring (Thur-Sun 10am-2pm & 5-8pm) or at Caja de Madrid (☎ 902 48 84 88).

Cycling
La Vuelta de España (Tour of Spain) finishes its spoke-fest in Madrid (having started three weeks before in Valencia) on the last Sunday of September. In 2002, riders peddled to Estadio Santiago Bernabeu to decide who was best at touring Spain on two wheels. For details, visit ⓔ www.lavuelta.com.

Football
The biggest spectator sport is, of course, football. Madrid's most glamorous team is Real Madrid, which plays at **Estadio Santiago Bernabéu** (2, E6; ☎ 91 398 43 00 or 902 27 17 07; Paseo de la Castellana 144; Ⓜ Santiago Bernabéu). Other teams are Atlético de Madrid, which plays at **Estadio Vicente Calderón** (2, P2; ☎ 91 366 47 07; Calle de la Virgen del Puerto; Ⓜ Pirámides); and Rayo Vallecano, which plays at **Nuevo Estadio de Vallecas Teresa Rivero** (1, E4; ☎ 91 478 22 53; ⓔ www.rayovallecano.es; Avenida del Payaso Fofó, Vallecas; Ⓜ Portazgo) – with a reputation for a jovial atmosphere at their games. Tickets for a Real Madrid match will cost from €6 to €40, but can be hard to come by for important matches. Tickets can be bought from stadiums, from ticket offices on Calle de la Victoria or by phone on ☎ 902 32 43 24.

Real Ronaldo
In September 2002, all of Madrid heard the news it had been waiting for all summer. Yep, Ronaldo would play for Real Madrid. The most famous footballer in the world to play with the most famous team – a match made in heaven.

A mark of Real Madrid's success

Tennis
Madrid now plays host to the Tennis Masters series (which attracts big bucks and bigger names) in October. A new 9000-seat indoor hard court (2, P1; Calle de las Aves; Ⓜ Lago) named **Recinto Ferial** was under construction on the site of the old Rocódomo in Casa de Campo in August 2002. For more information go to ⓔ www.tennis-masters-madrid.com. Tickets can be purchased from both El Corte Inglés (☎ 902 400 222) or Servicaixa (☎ 902 332 211).

places to stay

Madrid has plenty of places to stay, and plenty of visitors wanting to stay. There are good hotels in every price bracket, but it can be wise to book ahead, as Madrid's capital status makes it a mecca for business travellers and tourists alike.

Madrid has many excellent deluxe hotels that will have you wanting to move in permanently. Styles vary between state-of-the-art minimalist lodgings (straight from the pages of *wallpaper**) to old-world five-star palaces slathered in gilt and laden with chandeliers. Sadly, there's a noticeable decline in imagination from top end hotels – with a grand-but-bland ethos seeming to rule the roost. Madrid's mid-range places often have endearingly kitsch touches clearly intended to inject a bit of 'class' into the lobby or rooms, but frequently remain in the 'try-hard' league. Madrid's budget hotels are often in the noisier parts of town, but while rooms are usually simple, they are generally spotless, with lots of mop-and-bucket work going on every morning.

Accommodation comes in two categories: hotels (H), and *hostales* (Hs; cheap to mid-range hotels), with signs indicating each place's status. All hotels are subject to the 7% value-added tax known as IVA.

Room Rates

The prices in this chapter indicate the cost per night of a standard double room and are intended as a guide only. The reviews assess the character and facilities of each place within the context of the price bracket.

Deluxe	over €200
Top End	€100-200
Mid-Range	€45-99
Budget	under €45

Room with a view at the Hotel Atlántico (p104)

DELUXE

Hesperia Hotel
(4, F8) When a hotel's list of attributes includes a beautiful interior courtyard, one of the city's greatest restaurants and a piano bar with 'Madrid's widest selection of whiskies', then you hardly have to worry about an unpleasant surprise. Everything is good here – from the service to the design (handled by Pasqua Ortega, who remodelled the Teatro Real).

✉ **Paseo de la Castellana 57, Chamberi** ☎ **91 210 88 00 fax 91 210 88 99** ℮ **www.hesperia-madrid.com** Ⓜ **Gregorio Marañón** ✕ **see Santceloni p75**

Hotel Abascal (4, F6)
An ex-embassy building, and mighty attractive to boot, this hotel has been given a modern fit-out that thankfully retains some of the charming period details of its previous incarnation. A good Basque restaurant and a great summer terrace distinguish it from other big business hotels.

✉ **Calle de José Abascal 47, Ríos Rosas**

☎ **91 441 00 15 fax 91 442 22 11** ℮ **nhabas cal@nh-hoteles.es** Ⓜ **Alonso Cano** ✕

Hotel Bauzá (2, L8)
Hotel Bauzá opened in 1999 and revels in its own modern beauty. Everything is stunning here, with not an inch of chintz or a hint of ruffle. Rooms are beautifully decorated and include lots of little luxuries, though we're still not sure what the 'interactive TV' is. But we like the pillow menu!

✉ **Calle de Goya 79, Salamanca** ☎ **91 435 75 45 fax 91 431 09 43** ℮ **www.hotelbauza.com** Ⓜ **Goya** ✕

Hotel Emperatriz
(4, G9) Close to the shopping of Salamanca and with helpful, multilingual staff, the Emperatriz is just dandy for those looking for luxury or needing a place with good business facilities. The lounge areas and rooms are attractive.

✉ **Calle López de Hoyos 4, Castellana** ☎ **91 563 80 88 fax 91 563 98 04**

℮ **www.hotel-emperatriz.com** Ⓜ **Gregorio Marañón** ✕ ❄

Hotel Ritz (3, G14)
The Ritz opened its doors in 1920 under the watchful eye of both King Alfonso XIII and Cesar Ritz, and there's no chance of standards slipping as it approaches 100 years of ritziness. Even the sheets (hand-embroidered) are luxurious; business and fitness facilities are excellent.

✉ **Plaza de la Lealtad 5, Retiro** ☎ **91 701 67 67 fax 91 701 67 76** ℮ **www.ritz.es** Ⓜ **Banco de España** ✕ **Goya** ♨

Hotel Villa Magna
(4, J9) Visually unappealing from the exterior, this place's interior marks it as a five-star festival. Got a rock star with a troublesome hooker in the bathroom? This place can manage it without batting an eyelid. Business people and fitness fanatics are looked after royally too.

✉ **Paseo de la Castellana 22, Salamanca** ☎ **91 587 12 34 fax 91 431 22 86** ℮ **hotel@villamagna.es** Ⓜ **Rubén Darío** ✕ **see Le Divellec p85** ♨ ♿

Hotel Villa Real
(3, G12) Salivating, we decided that this was *the* place to stay if you wanted to absorb both art's Golden Triangle and the nightlife of Huertas and Santa Ana. Service is bend-over-backwards gracious, with everything you could hope

Ritzy Hotel Ritz

The grand Westin Palace Hotel

for, all provided in an enchanting, art-filled setting that manages to avoid the clichés.
✉ **Plaza de las Cortes 10, Huertas** ☎ **91 420 37 67 fax 91 420 25 47** e **villareal@derby hotels.es** Ⓜ **Banco de España** ✕ see East 47 p79 ♿

Santo Mauro (4, J7)
A stunning hotel, we were seriously tempted to move into the Santo Mauro when told 'is your house' as we were shown the tasteful modern rooms, beautifully renovated common areas, an indoor swimming pool and a delightful garden area where late suppers are served. Sigh.
✉ **Calle de Zurbano 36, Chamberí** ☎ **91 319 69 00 fax 91 308 54 77** e **santo-mauro@ ac-hoteles.com** Ⓜ **Rubén Darío or Alonso Martínez** ✕ see Santo Mauro p76 ♿

Tryp Reina Victoria
(3, H10) Something of a bullfighters' haunt, this place is really quite soul-less when you take the aforementioned titbit away, but it's smoothly run and

has been restored to wedding-cake glory (along with the sanitised Plaza de Santa Ana).
✉ **Plaza de Santa Ana 14, Santa Ana** ☎ **91 531 45 00 fax 91 522 03 07** e **tryp.reina .victoria@solmelia.com** Ⓜ **Sol or Sevilla** ✕

Westin Palace
(3, G13) Commissioned by none other than King Alfonso XIII himself (who wanted a comfortable place for his wedding guests to stay), this

elegant hotel, built in 1910 on the site of the former palace of the Duque de Lerma, has not let up on the luxury since. No detail has been overlooked, and we love the stunning stained-glass dome, the fancy bathrooms and the sheer 'marblelousness' of the 465-room palace.
✉ **Plaza de las Cortes 7, Cortes** ☎ **91 360 80 00 fax 91 360 81 00** e **www.westin.com** Ⓜ **Banco de España** ✕ **La Cupola or La Rotonda** ♿

Tryp Reina Victoria, Plaza Santa Ana

TOP END

Gran Hotel Conde Duque (4, J2)
Set on a quiet, tree-filled plaza, the Conde Duque appeals to business travellers because of its location and excellent service. Great deals can be negotiated for weekends, and the restaurant has Basque cuisine. Single rooms are very small – doubles are dandy.
✉ **Plaza del Conde Valle Suchil 5, Chamberí** ☎ **91 447 70 00 fax 91 448 35 69** e **www .hotelcondeduque.es** Ⓜ **San Bernardo or Quevedo** ✕

Hotel Alcalá (2, L7)
Despite its size, this hotel retains quite an intimate atmosphere, with kind staff at the front desk and some unusual touches, such as seven suites designed by *movida* queen-turned-fashion-designer Agatha Ruiz de la Prada (remember

to wear your sunglasses!). The other rooms are smart, but may be considered a little tame by comparison.
✉ **Calle de Alcalá 66, Retiro** ☎ **91 435 10 60 fax 91 435 11 05** e **www.nh-hoteles.es** Ⓜ **Príncipe de Vergara** ✕ ⚄

Hotel Atlántico (3, E9)
The exterior of this hotel resembles a glorious *belle époque* wedding cake. Designed by Joaquín Saldaña in 1920, this place reflects Madrid's and Gran Vía's architectural heyday. The interior? By contrast to the outside, it's subdued, functional and comfortable, with all the mod cons (gym and lounge) and some great views.
✉ **Gran Vía 38, Gran Vía** ☎ **91 522 64 80 fax 91 531 02 10** e **www.hotelatlantico .es** Ⓜ **Gran Vía** ✕ ⚄

Hotel Campomanes (3, F7)
A stylish and well-managed addition to Madrid's hotel scene, the Campomanes has a black--and-white decor and a subdued coolness to all of its 30 rooms. A very slick package indeed, in a prime location for sightseeing.
✉ **Calle de Campomanes 4,** ☎ **91 548 85 48 fax 91 559 12 88** e **www.hhcam pomanes.com** Ⓜ **Ópera** ✕ ⚄

Hotel Carlos V (3, F9)
This is a plushly renovated 67-room hotel with a distinctive, old-fashioned (despite all the mod-cons) feel – right down to the suit of armour in the lobby. The hotel also has a rooftop area – the perfect spot for a leisurely breakfast on a sunny day.
✉ **Calle del Maestro Victoria 5, Sol**

Making waves at Hotel Emperador (p105)

☎ 91 531 41 00
fax 91 531 37 61
e recepción@hotel
carlosv.com **Ⓜ** Sol or
Callao ✕

Hotel Don Pío (2, C8)

Located in the city's north, and totally nondescript from the outside, the Don Pío is quite a surprise inside. There's some very delicate woodwork in evidence and a welcome feeling of space, especially in the central patio area. Business facilities are very good too, and the hotel has parking and fantastic bathtubs to boot.
✉ **Avenida Pío XII 25, Chamartín** ☎ 91 353 07 80 fax 91 353 07 81 **Ⓜ** Pío XII ✕ ♿

Hotel Emperador

(3, D8) With rooms full of sumptuous flourishes, this is an ideal place to conduct business if you're out to impress. Quiet, despite the raucous Gran Vía below, you can chill out after a stint in a conference room by swimming in the great rooftop pool, which has city views.
✉ **Gran Vía 53, Gran Vía** ☎ 91 547 28 00 fax 91 547 28 17 **e** www.emperador hotel.com **Ⓜ** Callao or Santo Domingo ✕

Hotel Ópera (3, F7)

A strange one this: the location and standards are excellent, and there's nothing to complain about on the decor front, except for the fact that there are no double rooms here – only twins are available. This might be hard for loving couples, but fine for estranged opera buffs.
✉ **Cuesta de Santo Domingo 2, Los Austrias** ☎ 91 541 28 00 fax 91 541 69 23 **e** www.hotelopera .com **Ⓜ** Ópera ✕ yes, but with singing waiters! ♿

Hotel Suecia (3, F13)

They say: 'We just want to be the nicest' – and they *are* extremely nice here, right down to providing comfortable chairs for those waiting for a taxi. Room standards are high (and particularly good for business travellers), and Hemingway even stayed here in the 1950s.
✉ **Calle Marqués de Casa Riera 4** ☎ 91 531 69 00 fax 91 521 71 41 **e** www.hotelsuecia. com **Ⓜ** Banco de España ✕ yes ♿

Breakfast Included

Many *madrileños* aren't big on breakfast, with a coffee and a pastry deemed a sufficient way to start the day. This is one reason to avoid paying exorbitant rates for hotel breakfasts served by a certain hour. Even if they are included in the room rates, they're generally pretty desultory affairs, and not worth the effort. Get outside and go to a café instead.

Coffee at Plaza de Santa Ana

Those Precious Zzzzzs

You'll wonder if anyone sleeps in Madrid, and may well go way past your bedtime most nights, but if you're counting on some real shut-eye, it might be wise to avoid hotel rooms that face the street in Madrid's nightlife *barrios* (neighbourhoods). When you add the noise of revelry to the late-night garbage collection, early-morning street cleaning and roadworks, sirens, church bells, barking dogs, howling kids and arguing couples, you get quite a decibel cocktail. Light sleepers beware! Deluxe and top-end hotels will be more familiar with double-glazing on windows than will mid-range and budget hotels.

Yes, you're still in Madrid – Hotel París

MID-RANGE

Hostal La Macarena (3, H7) Housed in a well-groomed building on the western side of Plaza Mayor, this efficient, safe place offers smallish rooms, with bathroom, TV and air-con, plus a hard-to-beat position for those who love this part of town.
✉ Cava de San Miguel 8 ☎ 91 365 92 21 fax 91 366 61 11 Ⓜ Sol ✗ see Los Austrias pp82–4

Hostal Madrid (3, G9) A real find in this category, the Madrid has with-it management who are really helpful, while the rooms

(less than 20) are a definite cut above the usual, with TV, air-con, phone, hairdryer and safe. You can also self-cater in their mini-apartments, although the proximity to restaurants might put paid to that.
✉ Calle de Esparteros 6, Los Austrias ☎ 91 522 00 60 fax 91 532 35 10 Ⓜ Sol ✗ see Los Austrias pp82–4

Hostal Persal (3, H10) This place is a lot better than many *hostales*, and even many hotels The Persal is very well run and has clean, simple rooms with bathroom in a central

location. Sometimes Plaza del Ángel can be a little boozy late at night, but it's harmless stuff and you might just sleep through it.
✉ Plaza del Ángel 12, Huertas ☎ 91 369 46 43 fax 91 369 19 52 ⓔ hostal.persal @mad.servicom.es Ⓜ Sol or Antón Martín ✗ see Huertas & Santa Ana pp78–81

Hostal Sonsoles (3, D11) Close to the non-stop party that is Chueca, this gay-friendly two-star *hostal* has pretty good rooms, with bathroom, phone, TV and safe. On top

of this, they can put you in the know about gay venues and they certainly won't have any curfew hang-ups.
✉ **Calle de Fuencarral 18, Chueca** ☎ **91 532 75 23 fax 91 532 75 22** e **sonsodesa@eresmas .net** Ⓜ **Gran Vía** ✕ see **Chueca pp76–8**

Hotel Europa (3, F10)
With a pleasant little plant-filled courtyard in its centre and some rather alarming synthetic flowers throughout the premises, this place is cute – in a kitsch way. It's also incredibly close to the Puerta del Sol, located on a pedestrianised street, and has decent food in its restaurant.
✉ **Calle del Carmen 4, Sol** ☎ **91 521 29 00 fax 91 521 46 96** e **www.hoteleuropa .net** Ⓜ **Sol** ✕

Hotel Miau (3, H11)
If you want to be close to the nightlife of Plaza de Santa Ana, then this is the place for you. Newly opened in 2002, a genuine effort has been made (with much success) to offer a truly smart alternative to some of the scruffier places in the area. Still, it's a noisy district.
✉ **Calle del Principe 26, Santa Ana** ☎ **91 369 71 20 fax 91 429 72 37** Ⓜ **Antón Martín** ✕ see **Huertas & Santa Ana pp78–81**

Hotel Mónaco (3, D12) Tell us a place used to be a brothel and we'll want a peek. The laughably kitsch lobby (with indifferent staff) is just a taster, and the rooms (one equipped with a mirrored canopy) are perfect for amateur filmmaking of the trashiest order.
✉ **Calle de Barbieri 5, Chueca** ☎ **91 522 46 30 fax 91 521 16 01** Ⓜ **Gran Vía or Chueca** ✕ see **Chueca pp76–8**

Hotel Mora (3, K14)
This is a good choice in this category, with proximity to the 'big three' and Atocha station a bonus. Rooms are similar to so many others we've seen in Madrid, but you'll get satellite TV, air-con, phone and a tub.
✉ **Paseo del Prado 32, Huertas** ☎ **91 420 15 69 fax 91 420 05 64** Ⓜ **Atocha** ✕

Hotel París (3, G10)
With just a touch of faded grandeur, this hotel, smack-bang on the Puerta del Sol and situated under the famous Tío Pepe sign, is a good choice in this area. Rooms have TV, phone, air-con and a lot of fabric details, and the staff are helpful.
✉ **Calle de Alcalá 2, Sol** ☎ **91 521 54 91 fax 91 531 01 88** Ⓜ **Sol** ✕ see **Sol & Gran Vía p87**

BUDGET

Hostal Cantábrico (3, G11) The clean rooms here look a little uninspired in terms of decor, but by and large, this place has a charming air, thanks to the tiles. There's a nice little patio for dining as well, if you can't be bothered choosing from the hundreds of options in the area.
✉ **Calle de la Cruz 5, Huertas** ☎ **91 531 01 30 fax 91 532 14 41** Ⓜ **Sevilla** ✕

Hostal Cruz Sol (3, G9) On the 3rd floor (hooray for the lift!) of a building that's showing its age, the Cruz Sol, with its immaculately tidy rooms (including bathroom, TV and phone) comes as a pleasant surprise. The staff's kindness is another plus.
✉ **Plaza de Santa Cruz 6, Los Austrias** ☎/fax **91 532 71 97** e **www.hostalcruz sol.com** Ⓜ **Sol** ✕ see **Los Austrias pp82–4**

Hostal Dulcinea (3, H13) In a location close to Plaza de Santa Ana, but quiet enough to let you get some shut-eye, the spotlessly clean Dulcinea is a great choice in this range. The owners are courteous and helpful; if it's full they

Budget beds

No fuss San Antonio

floors and a busy-bee approach to cleanliness only reinforce the feeling. Rooms are simple and bathrooms sparkle.
✉ **Calle de Fuencarral 20, Chueca ☎ 91 531 63 00 fax 91 531 63 09 e www.iespana.es/ hostalmariacristina Ⓜ Gran Vía ✕ see Chueca pp76–8 ♿**

Hostal Retiro (2, L8) With a dose of greenery – thanks to the nearby Parque del Buen Retiro – and friendly management, this is the only real way to adhere to this price bracket in this tonier part of town. The rooms are comfortable and in good nick, particularly on the 4th floor, although short on luxuries.
✉ **Calle de O'Donnell 27, Retiro ☎ 91 576 00 37 Ⓜ Príncipe de Vergara or Ibiza ✕ see Salamanca & Retiro pp85–7 ♿**

Hostal San Antonio (3, H12) A handy place with tidy air-con rooms (all including bathroom) and helpful, straightforward service, the San Antonio gets good recommendations, although Calle de León itself can get *choked* with traffic (pedestrian and vehicular) until the wee hours on weekends.
✉ **Calle de León 13, Huertas ☎ 91 429 51 37 Ⓜ Antón Martín ✕ see Huertas & Santa Ana pp78–81 ♿**

Hostal Sardinero (3, H12) A stone's throw from beer-loving Plaza de Santa Ana, this 3rd-floor *hostal* has pleasant, handy rooms with air-con, safe, TV and bathroom, although

can direct you to their other property across the street.
✉ **Calle de Cervantes 19, Huertas ☎ 91 429 93 09 fax 91 369 25 69 e donato@teleline.es Ⓜ Antón Martín ✕ see Huertas & Santa Ana pp78–81**

Hostal Maria Cristina (3, D11) After the hustle of Calle de Fuencarral and a flight of stairs, the lobby – which resembles your grandma's living room in the 1970s – is quite comforting. Creaky parquet

you'll want to ask for a quiet room, bring some earplugs or keep *madrileño* social hours.
✉ **Calle del Prado 16, Santa Ana ☎ 91 429 57 56 fax 91 429 41 12 Ⓜ Sol or Antón Martín ✕ see Huertas & Santa Ana pp78–81 ♿**

Hostal Sil & Serranos (3, A10) These two *hostales*, which are under the same management (go to the 2nd floor), have rooms that are nudging their way out of the budget category. The standards are high, with air-con, phone and satellite TV in well-maintained rooms. They're also close to Chueca's and Malasaña's nightlife, without being in the thick of it.
✉ **Calle de Fuencarral 95, Malasaña ☎ 91 448 89 72 fax 91 447 48 29 Ⓜ Bilbao ✕ see Malasaña & Around pp84–5 ♿**

Children & Hospitality

Apart from top-end and deluxe places, which cater to every whim, Madrid's hotels don't go overboard with family-friendly details. There are often many flights of stairs (or tiny elevators with no room for a pram) and the nightlife outside is generally unmuffled. You can ask for children's cots, and they'll be provided in some places, but it's best to look for the ♿ in our reviews.

facts for the visitor

Cars, bars and plazas

ARRIVAL & DEPARTURE

As the capital of Spain, Madrid is easily accessible by air from anywhere in Europe and North America. The city is also linked to its European neighbours and Morocco by train and bus (more arduous and often no cheaper than flying). Plenty of air, rail and road connections link Madrid to the rest of the country.

Air

Madrid's Barajas airport (1, E4) is 13km northeast of the city centre. There are three terminals: T1 mostly handles intercontinental and some European flights; T2 mostly handles domestic and Schengen-country flights with Spanish carriers; and T3 handles Iberia's Puente Aereo flights between Madrid and Barcelona.

Left Luggage

The *consigna* (left luggage) offices are in T1 (near the bus stop & taxi stand) and T2 (near the metro entrance). Both are open 24hrs and charge €2.60 for 24hrs.

Information

General Inquiries
☎ 91 393 60 00

Flight Information
☎ 902 35 35 70

Hotel Booking Service
☎ 91 305 84 19

Airport Access

There are two main **parking** areas, both short and long term: P1 (outside T1), and P2 (outside T2); the first 30mins are free.

The recently opened **metro** line (No 8) between Barajas and Nuevos Ministerios (4, C8) is the easiest way to travel between the airport and the city. The trip takes 12mins and from here you can easily connect to your final destination. See Metro (p112) for general times and ticket costs.

The airport **bus** (No 89) runs between the airport and central Madrid. It arrives at and departs from an underground terminus at Plaza de Colón (3, B15). The bus runs from 5.15am to 2am daily every 12mins and costs €2.40 one way. The trip takes about 30mins in average traffic.

A **taxi** to/from the airport costs between €15 and €18. Taxis queue outside all three airport terminals.

Train

Madrid's two main train stations are Atocha (2, O6) and Chamartín (2, A7) in the city's south and north respectively. Atocha is the bigger of the two and the majority of trains to/from the south and east of Spain use this station, while international services arrive at and depart from Chamartín.

The variety of fares and services is mind-boggling. National trains are run by Renfe (☎ 902 24 02 02; e www.renfe.es) and tickets can be purchased by phone, online, at stations and at the Renfe booking office (3, F13; Calle de Alcalá 44; open Mon-Fri 9.30am-8pm).

Bus

The main intercity bus terminal is Estación Sur de Autobuses (☎ 91 468 42 00; e www.estaciondeauto buses.com; Calle de Méndez Álvaro), just south of the M-30 ring road. It serves most destinations to the south and many in other parts of the country. Most bus companies have a ticket office here, even if their buses depart from elsewhere.

Herranz buses (2, J2; ☎ 91 896 90 28) depart from under and around Moncloa station for El Escorial and El Pardo.

The major international carrier is Eurolines (ⓔ www.eurolines.com), which often works in tandem with Spanish carriers that depart from or arrive at Estación Sur de Autobuses.

Travel Documents

Passport

Spain is one of 15 countries that are party to the Schengen agreement, and there is usually no passport control for people arriving from within the EU – although you must carry your passport or a national ID card.

Visa

Visas are not required by citizens of the EU, USA, Australia, Canada, New Zealand, Israel, Japan and Switzerland for tourist visits to Spain of up to three months. If you are a citizen of a country not listed here, check with your Spanish consulate before you travel, as you may need a specific visa. If you intend to stay for more than three months you must apply for a resident's card.

Return/Onward Ticket

A return/onward ticket makes entry into Spain easier for non-EU citizens.

Customs & Duty Free

From outside the EU, you can bring in one bottle of spirits, one bottle of wine, 50mL of perfume and 200 ciggies. From an EU country (with duty paid) you can bring in 90L of wine, 10L of spirits, unlimited perfume and 800 ciggies, and really make a party of it.

Departure Tax

Departure tax is pre-paid with your ticket.

GETTING AROUND

Madrid's public transport is reliable, efficient and user-friendly. The metro is by far the best way to get around town; it stops close to most places of interest and doesn't smell like an underground urinal. The metro is complemented by the Cercanías suburban rail system, and an extensive network of local buses.

The main transport system finishes at around 1.30am, which means you'll sometimes need to use taxis to get the most out of Madrid's famed nightlife. And Madrid being Madrid, it can be harder to get a taxi at 4am than 4pm! Maps of Madrid's transport network are available from tourist offices, train and metro stations, and the airport.

Travel Passes

Monthly or season passes (*abonos*) are only worth buying if you're staying long term and using local transport frequently. You'll also need an ID card (*carnet*), available from metro stations and tobacconists. Take a passport-sized photo and your passport. A monthly ticket for central Madrid (Zona A) costs €32.30 and is valid for unlimited travel on bus, metro and Cercanías trains.

Metro

Madrid's excellent metro system (see inside front cover; ☎ 902 44 44 03) has 11 colour-coded lines (with extra stops being added all the time!) and runs from about 6am to 1.30am daily. You can buy tickets from staffed kiosks or machines at the stations; a single trip costs 95c or a Metrobús ticket (valid for 10 trips) costs €5. Only some of the newer stations have wheelchair access.

Bus

Buses run by Empresa Municipal de Transportes de Madrid (EMT, ☎ 91 406 88 10) travel regularly along 170 lines, covering most city routes, between 6.30am and 11.30pm daily. A single-trip ticket costs 95c and a Metrobús ticket (valid for 10 trips) costs €5. About half of the buses are *piso bajo* types, meaning they are wheelchair-friendly.

Cercanías

These short-range regional trains are handy for making north–south trips between Chamartín and Atocha stations, and for places like El Escorial and Aranjuez. As this system is operated by Renfe, the national rail network, tickets (single-trip 90c) are not valid on buses or the metro, although most international rail passes are valid.

Taxi

Madrid's taxis (white with a diagonal red stripe) are plentiful and good value compared to other European cities. Make sure the driver turns the meter on; flag fall is €1.35 plus 63c per kilometre (81c between 10pm and 6am). On public holidays it's 81c per kilometre (91c between 10pm and 6am).

Supplementary charges include: €4 to/from the airport, €2 from cab ranks at train and bus stations, €2 for travelling to/from Parque Juan Carlos I, and a special charge on Christmas Eve and New Year's Eve.

A green light on the roof, or a sign displayed behind the windscreen with the word '*libre*' means the taxi is available. You can book taxis with:

Radio-Taxi Independiente	☎ 91 405 12 13
Radio Teléfono	☎ 91 547 82 00
Teletaxi	☎ 91 371 21 31

Car & Motorcycle

Trying to find a park in Madrid will give your thesaurus of swearwords a workout. And driving will be frustrating, not because of the other drivers (although they don't seem to prize road rules much) but for the maze of one-way narrow streets in the older parts of town. The risk of car theft is another deterrent. Motorcycles and scooters are popular modes of transport, but Madrid is not the place to learn how to ride them!

Petrol prices vary, but count on paying about 80c per litre for lead-free (*sin plomo*), 86c for Super 97 (a lead-replacement petrol) or 68c for diesel (*gasóleo*).

Road Rules

Driving takes place on the right-hand side of the road and seatbelts are compulsory, with on-the-spot fines for the unbuckled.

Speed limits are as follows: on *autovías* (motorways) 120km/h; on highways 100km/h; on other roadways 90km/h; on urban streets 50km/h; and in residential areas 20km/h. It's illegal to drive with a blood-alcohol content of 0.05% or higher.

Rental

Car hire is relatively expensive in Madrid and generally ill-advised unless you're planning more than a couple of day trips. All the major car companies have offices in Madrid and at the airport, although smaller firms such as Julià Car (☎ 91 779 18 60) are a bit cheaper. With a firm such as Hertz (3, C6; ☎ 902 40 24 05; Edificio de España, Plaza de España) you're looking at about €136 for their best three-day weekend deal including insurance and 400km per day.

You can rent motorcycles from Moto Alquiler (☎ 91 542 06 57; Calle del Conde Duque 13) costing €360 for a Monday-to-Friday deal, with a €1500 deposit on your credit card.

Driving Licence & Permit

EU member states' pink-and-green driving licences are recognised in Spain. If you hold a licence from another country you are supposed to obtain an International Driving Permit (IDP).

Motoring Organisations

The head office of the Real Automóvil Club de España (RACE; 4, H5; ☎ 902 30 05 05; Calle de Eloy Gonzalo 32) is in Madrid. Its 24hr, countrywide emergency breakdown service is free for RACE members. Your own national motoring organisation may have reciprocal arrangements with RACE. You will generally be provided with a special telephone number to use in an emergency while in Spain.

PRACTICAL INFORMATION

Climate & When to Go

Madrid's continental climate brings scorching hot summers and dry, cold winters. Locals say *'nueve meses de invierno y tres de infierno'* (nine months of winter and three months of hell). This is a slight exaggeration, but the message is clear that at its worst, Madrid can be nastily cold and infernally hot.

July and August are hottest, with temperatures frequently over 30°C and sometimes over 40°C. In winter, temperatures can plummet to freezing at night and might only nudge 10°C during the day. Late April and May are lovely times to visit, as are September and early October (although this month can be rainy). February can be surprisingly nice, with blue skies and sun.

March is often unpredictable, and early April can be wet.

The combination of tourists and business travellers visiting Madrid means that hotels are busy for much of the year. The city is

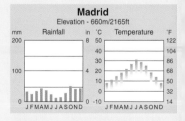

Madrid
Elevation - 660m/2165ft

especially crowded during Easter, Christmas holidays and local festivals. Many *madrileños* take holidays in August, which means that the city is noticeably less crowded.

Tourist Information

Tourist Information Abroad

Information on Madrid is available from the following branches of the Oficina Española de Turismo:

Canada
2 Bloor St W, 34th floor, Toronto M4W 3E2 (☎ 416-961 3131; 🔘 toronto@tourspain.es)

France
43 rue Decamps, 75784 Paris Cedex 16 (☎ 01 45 03 82 57; fax 01 45 03 82 51; 🔘 paris@tourspain.es)

Germany
Kurfüdamm 63, D-10707, Berlin (☎ 030-882 6543; 🔘 berlin@tourspain.es)

Portugal
Avenida Sídonio Pais 28, 1050 Lisbon (☎ 21-354 1992; 🔘 lisboa@tourspain.es)

UK
22-3 Manchester Square, London W1U 3PX (☎ 020-7486 8077; 🔘 londres@tourspain.es)

USA
666 Fifth Ave, 35th floor, New York, NY 10103 (☎ 212-265 8822; 🔘 nyork@tourspain.es)

Local Tourist Information

The tourist offices in the city have friendly staff who speak English (among other languages) and can provide maps and information about Madrid and its environs. The email addresses for all the offices (except Plaza Mayor) is 🔘 turismo@comadrid.es. The Patronato Municipal de Turismo specialises in Madrid-only information. In summer, bright yellow kiosks are established around well-touristed city points, with multilingual staff.

Aeroporto de Barajas
Ground fl, T1 (1, E4; ☎ 91 305 86 56; 8am-8pm)

Estación de Chamartín
Estación de Chamartín (2, A7; ☎ 91 315 99 76; Mon-Sat 8am-8pm, Sun & hols 9am-3pm)

Estación Puerta de Atocha
Estación Puerta de Atocha (2, O6; ☎ 902 100 007; 9am-9pm)

Mercado Puerta de Toledo
Ronda de Toledo 1, Stand 3134 (2, O3; ☎ 91 364 18 76; Mon-Sat 9am-7pm, Sun & hols 9am-3pm)

Oficina de Turismo Duque de Medinaceli
Calle del Duque de Medinaceli 2 (3, H13; ☎ 91 429 37 05; Mon-Sat 9am-7pm, Sun & hols 9am-3pm)

Patronato Municipal de Turismo
Plaza Mayor 3 (3, H8; ☎ 91 588 16 36; 🔘 inforturismo@munimadrid.es; Mon-Sat 10am-8pm, Sun & hols 10am-3pm)

Embassies

Australia
Plaza del Descubridor Diego de Ordás 3-2, Edificio Santa Engrácia 120 (4, E5; ☎ 91 441 60 25; 🔘 www.spain.embassy.gov.au)

Canada
Calle de Núñez de Balboa 35 (2, L7; ☎ 91 423 3250; 🔘 www.canadaes.org)

France
Calle de Salustiano Olózaga 9 (3, E15; ☎ 91 423 89 00; 🔘 www.ambafrance-es.org)

Germany
Calle de Fortuny 8 (4, J8; ☎ 91 557 90 00; 🔘 www.embajada-alemania.es)

New Zealand
Plaza de la Lealtad 2 (3, G14; ☎ 91 523 02 26; fax 91 531 09 97)

UK
Calle de Fernando el Santo 16 (3, A14; ☎ 91 700 82 72)

USA
Calle de Serrano 75 (4, H9; ☎ 91 587 22 00; fax 91 587 23 83; 🔘 www.embusa.es)

Money

Currency

The unit of currency is the euro. Notes come in denominations of €500, €200, €100, €50, €20, €10 and €5. Coins come in denominations of €2 and €1, plus 50c, 20c, 10c, 5c, 2c and 1c.

Travellers Cheques

Travellers cheques are useful as they can be replaced if lost or stolen. American Express and Thomas Cook are widely accepted brands. You'll need your passport to cash them; see Changing Money below for more details.

Credit Cards

Credit cards are widely accepted throughout the city. Some places will want to see another form of photo ID, such as a passport or driving licence, but your signature will rarely be checked. For 24hr card cancellations or assistance, call:

American Express	☎ 902 37 35 37
Diners Club	☎ 91 547 74 00
MasterCard/Eurocard	☎ 900 97 12 31
Visa	☎ 900 97 44 45

ATMs

ATMs (*telebancos*) are common throughout Madrid, and as long as you're connected to the Cirrus or Maestro network, you're good to go. It usually works out cheaper than exchanging travellers cheques too, but check first with your bank at home for associated charges.

Changing Money

You can change cash or travellers cheques at most banks (Madrid is swarming with them) and at exchange offices, at bus and train stations and at the airport. Banks tend to offer the best rates, and most have ATMs. Exchange offices (mostly clustered around the Plaza de Puerta del Sol and along Gran Vía), usually indicated by the word *cambio* (exchange), offer longer opening hours and quicker service but have poorer exchange rates. Travellers cheques usually bring a slightly better rate than cash, but always check the commissions.

Bank opening hours are 8.30am-2pm Monday to Friday and 9am-1pm Saturday, although many banks don't bother opening on Saturday during summer.

Tipping

The law stipulates that restaurants include service charges in menu prices, so tipping is very much discretionary. Many people leave small change at bars and cafés (5% is plenty). Hotel porters will be happy with €1 and taxi drivers OK with a round-up.

Discounts

Concessions (up to 50%) are available for youths, students and seniors over 65 years (with identification) at most attractions and on some transport. The most widely recognised student and youth cards are the International Student Identity Card (ISIC) and the Carnet Joven Europeo (Euro <26 card). It's worth carrying photo ID and flashing it wherever possible to see what discounts (which are not always advertised) are available.

Travel Insurance

A policy covering theft, loss, medical expenses and compensation for cancellation or delays in your travel arrangements is highly recommended. If items are lost or stolen, make sure you get a police report straight away – otherwise your insurer might not pay up.

Opening Hours

Office hours are generally Monday to Friday from 9am to 2pm and then 5pm to 8pm. Shops keep similar hours, though they often open at 10am and also on Saturday; some big stores don't close for siesta. Restaurants tend to open from noon or 1pm to 4pm and then 8pm to midnight (after midnight on Friday and Saturday). Many shops close on Sunday, public holidays and for a few weeks in August.

Opening times for tourist sites vary. Museums tend to keep the same hours as shops (often without closing for lunch) but can have a shorter schedule in winter. Virtually all museums close on Monday, and many attractions are open shorter hours (or closed) in August.

Public Holidays

Jan 1	New Year's Day
Jan 6	Epiphany or Three Kings' Day
Mar/Apr	Good Thursday
Mar/Apr	Good Friday
May 1	Labour Day
May 2	El Dos de Mayo
Aug 15	Feast of the Assumption
Oct 12	Spanish National Holiday
Nov 1	All Saints' Day
Dec 8	Feast of the Immaculate Conception
Dec 25	Christmas Day

Time

Madrid is 1hr ahead of GMT/UTC and 2hrs ahead during daylight-savings. Daylight savings is observed for around seven months from the last Sunday in March to the last Sunday in October.

At noon in Madrid it's:

6am in New York
3am in Los Angeles
11am in London
1pm in Johannesburg
11pm in Auckland
9pm in Sydney

Electricity

Spain's electric current is 220V, 50Hz. If your appliances are geared for a different voltage, you'll need a transformer. Plugs are the two round-pin type, so you may also need an adaptor. Adaptors and transformers are best bought in your home country, although they are also stocked in many airport stores.

Weights & Measures

Spain uses the metric system. Decimal points are indicated with commas and thousands with points. See the conversion table (p122) for more details.

Post

Madrid's postal service is reliable and efficient. The main post office is in the Palacio de Comunicaciones (3, E14; Plaza de Cibeles; open Mon-Fri 8.30am-9.30pm & Sat 8.30am-2pm). Stamps are sold at most *estancos* (tobacconists – look for the sign with '*Tobacos*' in yellow letters on a maroon background), as well as post offices (*correos y telégrafos*).

Postal Rates

A standard postcard or letter weighing up to 20g costs 25c within Spain, 50c within Europe, and 75c to the Americas and Australasia. Aerograms cost 50c to anywhere in the world.

Opening Hours

Most post offices are open Mon-Fri 9am-2pm.

Telephone

The ubiquitous blue payphones are easy to use for both domestic and international calls. They accept coins, phonecards and sometimes credit cards.

Phonecards

Tarjetas telefónicas (phonecards) are sold at post offices, *estancos* (tobacconists) and many newsstands; they come in denominations of €5 and €10. Lonely Planet's ekno Communication Card, which is specifically aimed at travellers, provides competitive international calls (avoid using it for local calls), messaging services and free email. Log on to ☎ www.ekno.lonelyplanet.com for information on joining and accessing the service.

Mobile Phones

Spain uses the GSM cellular *(movil)* phone system, which works with most phones except those sold in the USA and Japan. To use your phone, you'll need to set up a global roaming service with your service provider before you leave home, or you can buy a Spanish SIM card for around €60.

Country & City Codes

Spain	☎ 34
Madrid	☎ 91

Useful Numbers

Local Directory Inquiries	☎ 1003
International Directory Inquiries	☎ 025
International Operator Europe/North Africa	☎ 1008
International Operator rest of the world	☎ 1005
Reverse-charge (collect) of the country you are calling)	☎ 900 (+ code
Time	☎ 093
Weather	☎ 906 36 53 28

International Direct Dial Codes

Dial ☎ 00 followed by:

Australia	☎ 61
Canada	☎ 15
Japan	☎ 81
New Zealand	☎ 64
South Africa	☎ 27
UK	☎ 44
USA	☎ 1

Digital Resources

Madrid has many Internet cafés, ranging in size from veritable telecommunications palaces with hundreds of terminals to small operations with half-a-dozen terminals. Many of the larger places to stay have facilities for guests for free or for a minimal fee.

Internet Service Providers

Major Internet service providers (ISPs) such as AOL (☎ www.aol.com), CompuServe (☎ www.compuserve.com) and AT&T Global (☎ www.attglobal.net) have dial-in nodes throughout Europe, including Madrid. Download a list of the dial-in numbers before you leave home.

Internet Cafés

If you can't access the Internet from where you're staying, head to a cybercafé:

easyEverything
Calle de Morena 10 (3, F10; ☎ www.easyeverything.com; open 24hrs; €1 for 30mins-2hrs)

3w.com
Calle de Tetuán 3 (3, F9; Mon-Sat 9-1am, Sun 11-1am; 60c for 30mins)

BBiGG
Calle de Alcalá 21 (3, F11; ☎ www.bbigg.com; Sun-Thur 9am-midnight, Fri & Sat 9am-2am; €1.20 per 30mins)

Useful Sites

The Lonely Planet website (**e** www.lonelyplanet.com) offers a speedy link to many of Madrid's websites. Others to try include:

Comunidad de Madrid
e www.comadrid.es

Descubre Madrid
e www.descubremadrid.com

Metro de Madrid
e www.metromadrid.es

Renfe
e www.renfe.es

Ayuntamiento de Madrid
e www.munimadrid.es

Doing Business

All the deluxe and top-end hotels have business facilities including conference rooms, secretarial services, fax machines and photocopiers, computers and private office space etc. If they don't provide translation services, they will know someone who does.

Your first port of call (apart from the trade office of your embassy or consulate) should be the Oficina de Congresos de Madrid (Madrid Convention Bureau; 3, H6; ☎ 91 588 29 00; fax 91 588 29 30; Patronato de Turismo office, Calle Mayor 69; open Mon-Fri 8am-3pm & 4-7pm).

Newspapers & Magazines

Madrid's main newspapers are *El País* and *El Mundo*. International newspapers, which include the *International Herald Tribune*, are available at newsstands around central Madrid, especially along Gran Vía and around Puerta del Sol. The *Guía del Ocio* (€1) is a must-read for anyone wanting to sample Madrid's entertainment options, and can be found at any newsstand. *Shangay* is Madrid's free gay paper and is available in many shops and bars, especially around the Chueca neighbourhood. *In Madrid* is a free English-language newspaper with good entertainment listings and classifieds. You can find it in bars and shops around the city.

Radio

BBC World Service broadcasts on a variety of frequencies (6195kHz, 9410kHz and 15,485kHz) depending on the time of day. Likewise, Voice of America can be found on short-wave frequencies at 6040kHz, 9760kHz and 15,205kHz. The Spanish national network, Radio Nacional de España (RNE), operates RNE1 (88.2FM) broadcasting general interest and current affairs. Classical music can be found at Sinfo Radio (104.3FM). For pop and rock, tune in to 40 Principales (93.9FM) or Onda Cero (98FM).

TV

State-run TVE1 and La 2 broadcast a combination of pro-government news, good arts programs and films. Antena 3 and Tele 5 are commercial stations sending out woeful soaps and 'all tits and teeth' variety shows. Canal Plus is a pay channel mostly devoted to film and football. Telemadrid broadcasts some football matches.

Photography & Video

Most brands of film are widely available and processing is efficient and of a decent standard. A roll of film (36 exposures, 100 ISO) costs around €4.50 and can be processed for around €12. For slide (*diapositiva*) film, you're looking at around €5.50 plus €5.20 for processing.

You can find developers all over

the city, including El Corte Inglés (p62) and FNAC (p61). For repairs, Playmon (2, L9; ☎ 91 573 57 25, Calle de Jorge Juan 133) has a good reputation, but your best bet is to look in the telephone directory for a specialist dealing in your make of equipment.

Spain uses the PAL video system, which is not compatible with other standards unless converted.

Health

Immunisations
There are no vaccination requirements for entry into Spain, although you may need to show proof of vaccination if you're coming from an area where yellow fever is endemic (Africa and South America).

Precautions
You should encounter no major health problems in Madrid. The water is potable, and health and hygiene standards are pretty good. The only problems you're likely to encounter are dehydration or sunburn and/or initial gut problems if you're unused to large quantities of olive oil. Pharmacists are generally quite sympathetic about dispensing most medicines without a prescription, although it's best to bring prescriptions for medication you are taking or may need.

Insurance & Medical Treatment
Travel insurance is advisable to cover any medical treatment you may need while in Madrid. Spain has reciprocal health agreements with other EU countries. Citizens of those countries need to get hold of an E111 form from their national health body. If you should require medical help you will need to present this, plus photocopies of

the form and your national health card.

Medical Services
Hospitals or *urgencias* (first-aid stations) with 24hr accident and emergency departments include:

Hospital General Gregorio Marañon
    Calle del Doctor Esquerdo (2, M9; ☎ 91 586 80 00; Ⓜ Sáinz de Baranda)
Centro de Salud
    Calle de la Navas de Tolosa 10 (3, E8; ☎ 91 521 00 25; Ⓜ Santo Domingo)
Hospital Clinico San Carlos
    Plaza del Cristo Rey (2, G2; ☎ 91 330 30 00; Ⓜ Moncloa)

Dental Services
If you chip a tooth or require emergency treatment, head to Clinica Dental Cisne (Calle de Magallanes 18; 4, H3; ☎ 91 446 32 21; 24hr emergency service).

Pharmacies
The following pharmacies are open 24hrs:

Farmacia del Globo
    Plaza de Antón Martín 46 (3, J11; ☎ 91 369 20 00)
Real Farmacia de la Reina
    Calle Mayor 59 (3, G7; ☎ 91 548 00 14)
Farmacia Velázquez
    Calle de Velázquez 70 (4, K10; ☎ 91 575 60 28)

Toilets

Public toilets are not common in Madrid. If you get caught short while sightseeing, you can pop into a bar or café, although some places might like you to buy a drink first.

Safety Concerns

Generally speaking, Madrid is very safe, although it's wise to keep a lookout for pickpockets on the metro and at major tourist attractions. Keep only a limited amount of cash on your person, and the bulk of your money in replaceable forms, such as travellers cheques or plastic; use your hotel's safe. Money or valuables that you need to take out with you should be securely concealed in a money belt. If you're carrying a bag, wear it across your body, not hanging from your shoulder.

Never leave anything in your car and don't get a hire car that has marking identifying it as such. Foreign number plates make you even more vulnerable.

Avoid anyone playing the old 'ball under the three cups' game, especially near Real Madrid's Estadio Santiago Bernabéu.

Lost Property

For the main lost property office (*Negociado de Objetos Perdidos*) call ☎ 91 588 43 46; things found on metro trains and in taxis are generally handed in here. For items lost on Renfe trains call ☎ 91 902 24 02 02. For the EMT bus network call ☎ 91 406 88 43. If you've lost something at the airport call ☎ 91 393 60 00.

Keeping Copies

Make photocopies of important documents, keep some with you – separate from the originals – and leave a copy at home. You can also store details of documents in Lonely Planet's free online Travel Vault; it's password-protected and it's accessible worldwide. See e www.ekno.lonelyplanet.com.

Emergency Numbers

Ambulance	☎ 061
Fire	☎ 080
Municipal Police	☎ 092
National Police	☎ 091
Rape Crisis	☎ 91 574 01 10

(open Mon-Fri 10am-2pm & 4-7pm)

Women Travellers

Despite Spain's chronic problem with domestic violence towards women, female visitors to Madrid will get the feeling that women's rights are respected. Lone women walking around late at night should encounter little troublesome attention, although the Lavapiés neighbourhood is best avoided in these circumstances.

Tampons and the contraceptive pill are widely available in Madrid at pharmacies – the RU-486 pill is another matter.

Gay & Lesbian Travellers

Madrid is very much a 'live and let live' city, and the gay and lesbian scene is out, loud and proud. Centred in the Chueca neighbourhood, but certainly not ghetto-ised, gay life here does not warrant furtive secrecy or segregation. In fact, it's fairly standard to see straight people in gay bars and clubs and gay people anywhere and everywhere. In Chueca though, you'll find bars, clubs, restaurants, shops and hotels that specifically cater to gay and lesbian customers.

Information & Organisations

The Colectivo de Gais y Lesbianas de Madrid (Cogam; 3, D10; ☎ 91 522 45 17; Calle de Fuencarral 37) has an information office and social centre and an information line (☎ 91 523 00 70). Fundación Triángulo (4, G5; ☎ 91 593 05 40; e www.fundaciontriangulo.es; Calle de Eloy Gonzalo 25) is another source of information on gay issues. Free publications worth picking up from the Chueca area include *Shangay*, *Shangay Express*, and *Mapa Gaya de Madrid*, which you can find at the Berkana bookshop (p61).

Senior Travellers

Madrid should present no major problems for senior travellers, although infernal summer heat may take its toll when combined with strenuous sightseeing time-tables. See also Discounts (p115).

Disabled Travellers

There are wheelchair-adapted taxis, buses and metro stations. The streets however, have not been designed with impaired mobility in mind. Many older museums don't have wheelchair access, although the 'big three' museums have been kitted out. Look for the ᵭ listed with individual reviews.

For deaf travellers, there are few concessions made in public infrastructure. There are some specially textured pavements at intersections for blind travellers, and some pedestrian crossing lights with sounded alternatives to the flashing green and red.

Information & Organisations

The Ayuntamiento de Madrid (see Useful Sites, p118) publishes a *Guia de Accesibilidad* that contains information on disabled access to everything from the city's cinemas to its public service buildings. It's designed more for disabled residents than visitors though. The Organización Nacional de Ciegos Españoles (ONCE; 4, J10; ☎ 91 577 37 56; Calle de José Ortega y Gasset 18) is the Spanish association for the blind.

Language

It's well worth the effort to try a few phrases in Spanish during your stay in Madrid, as English is not as widely spoken as many travellers may think. For an in-depth guide to the language, get a copy of Lonely Planet's *Spanish phrasebook*.

Basics

Hello	*¡Hola!*
Goodbye	*¡Adiós!*
Yes	*Sí*
No	*No*
Please	*Por favor*
Thank you	*Gracias*
You're welcome	*De nada*
OK/fine	*Vale*
Excuse me	*Perdón/ Perdone*
Sorry/Excuse me	*Losiento/ Discúlpeme*
Do you speak English?	*¿Habla inglés?*
I don't understand	*No Entiendo*
How much is it?	*¿Cuánto cuesta/vale?*
Where are the toilets?	*¿Dónde están los servicios?*
I'm a vegetarian	*Soy vegetariano/a*
Help!	*¡Socorro!/ ¡Auxilio!*

Days & Numbers

Monday	*lunes*
Tuesday	*martes*
Wednesday	*miércoles*
Thursday	*jueves*
Friday	*viernes*
Saturday	*sábado*
Sunday	*domingo*
0	*cero*
1	*uno, una*
2	*dos*
3	*tres*
4	*cuatro*
5	*cinco*
6	*seis*
7	*siete*
8	*ocho*
9	*nueve*
10	*diez*
100	*cien/ciento*
1000	*mil*

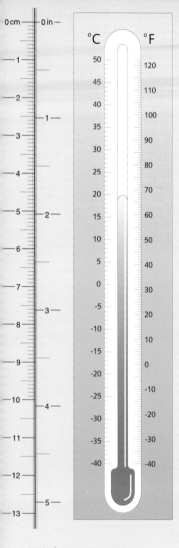

Conversion Table

Clothing Sizes

Measurements are approximate only; try before you buy.

Women's Clothing

Aust/NZ	8	10	12	14	16	18
Europe	36	38	40	42	44	46
Japan	5	7	9	11	13	15
UK	8	10	12	14	16	18
USA	6	8	10	12	14	16

Women's Shoes

Aust/NZ	5	6	7	8	9	10
Europe	35	36	37	38	39	40
France only	35	36	38	39	40	42
Japan	22	23	24	25	26	27
UK	3½	4½	5½	6½	7½	8½
USA	5	6	7	8	9	10

Men's Clothing

Aust/NZ	92	96	100	104	108	112
Europe	46	48	50	52	54	56
Japan	S		M	M		L
UK	35	36	37	38	39	40
USA	35	36	37	38	39	40

Men's Shirts (Collar Sizes)

Aust/NZ	38	39	40	41	42	43
Europe	38	39	40	41	42	43
Japan	38	39	40	41	42	43
UK	15	15½	16	16½	17	17½
USA	15	15½	16	16½	17	17½

Men's Shoes

Aust/NZ	7	8	9	10	11	12
Europe	41	42	43	44½	46	47
Japan	26	27	27.5	28	29	30
UK	7	8	9	10	11	12
USA	7½	8½	9½	10½	11½	12½

Weights & Measures

Weight

1kg = 2.2lb
1lb = 0.45kg
1g = 0.04oz
1oz = 28g

Volume

1 litre = 0.26 US gallons
1 US gallon = 3.8 litres
1 litre = 0.22 imperial gallons
1 imperial gallon = 4.55 litres

Length & Distance

1 inch = 2.54cm
1cm = 0.39 inches
1m = 3.3ft = 1.1yds
1ft = 0.3m
1km = 0.62 miles
1 mile = 1.6km

lonely planet

Lonely Planet is the world's most successful independent travel information company with offices in Australia, the USA, UK and France. With a reputation for comprehensive, reliable travel information, Lonely Planet is a print and electronic publishing leader, with over 650 titles and 22 series catering for travellers' individual needs.

At Lonely Planet we believe that travellers can make a positive contribution to the countries they visit – if they respect their host communities and spend their money wisely. Since 1986 a percentage of the income from books has been donated to aid and human rights projects.

www.lonelyplanet.com

For news, views and free subscriptions to print and email newsletters, and a full list of LP titles, click on Lonely Planet's award-winning website.

On the Town

A romantic escape to Paris or a mad shopping dash through New York City, the locals' secret bars or a city's top attractions – whether you have 24hrs to kill or months to explore, Lonely Planet's On the Town products will give you the low-down.

Condensed guides are ideal pocket guides for when time is tight. Their quick-view maps, full-colour layout and opinionated reviews help short-term visitors target the top sights and discover the very best eating, shopping and entertainment options a city has to offer.

For more indepth coverage, **City guides** offer insights into a city's character and cultural background as well as providing extensive coverage of where to eat, stay and play. **CitySync**, a digital guide for your handheld unit, allows you to reference stacks of opinionated, well-researched travel information. Portable and durable **City Maps** are perfect for locating those back-street bars or hard-to-find local haunts.

'Ideal for a generation of fast movers.'

– Gourmet Traveller on Condensed guides

Condensed Guides

- Amsterdam
- Athens
- Bangkok
- Barcelona
- Beijing (Sept 2003)
- Boston
- Brussels (March 2004)
- Chicago
- Dublin
- Florence (May 2003)
- Frankfurt
- Hong Kong
- Las Vegas (May 2003)
- London
- Los Angeles
- New Orleans
- New York City
- Paris
- Prague
- Rome
- San Francisco
- Singapore
- Sydney
- Tokyo
- Venice
- Washington, DC

index

See also separate indexes for Places to Eat (p. 126), Places to Stay (p. 127), Shops (p. 127) and Sights with map references (p. 128).

PLACES TO EAT